CONIECTANEA BIBLICA · NEW TESTAMENT SERIES 18

Aspects on the Johannine Literature

Papers presented at a conference of Scandinavian New Testament exegetes at Uppsala, June 16–19, 1986

Edited by Lars Hartman & Birger Olsson

Published with grants from the Swedish Council for Research in the Humanities and Social Sciences.

Abstract

Hartman, L., Olsson, B. (eds.), 1987. Aspects on the Johannine Literature. Papers presented at a conference of Scandinavian New Testament exegetes at Uppsala, June 16–19, 1986. *Coniectanea Biblica. New Testament Series 18*. 113 pp. Uppsala. ISBN 91-22-00929-9.

Seven papers deal with different problems of the New Testament Johannine literature: *K.-G. Sandelin*, The Johannine Writings within the Setting of their Cultural History, finds on the one hand a tendency towards isolation of the group(s) behind the texts, and on the other hand a usage of ideas and concepts from Greekspeaking Judaism which opens universal perspectives. *B. Olsson*, The History of the Johannine Movement, suggests a historical development of the "movement" which may be surmised behind the texts, not least the small Epistles. *Aa. Pilgaard*, The Gospel of John as Gospel Writing, discusses the relationship kerygma – gospel writing as applied to the Fourth Gospel. *T. Karlsen Seim*, Roles of Women in the Gospel of John, exposes what seems to be an explicit interest of the gospel, in that women, precisely *qua* women, play important roles as examples of discipleship. *R. Kieffer*, Different Levels in Johannine Imagery, sheds light on how the author of the gospel under its *significatum* – level seems constantly to presuppose a *significandum* – level (or an ideology) to be grasped by the Spirit-gifted reader. *L. Hartman*, Johannine Jesus-Belief and Monotheism, argues that the Logos Christology of the gospel was a means by which "the Johaninne Christian" could think of Jesus and his work as something "God-ly", but that the problem of what later theologians termed the two natures doctrine was not solved thereby. Finally, *H. Riesenfeld*, The Fourth Gospel as Viewed by Fridrichsen, Odeberg and Gyllenberg, describes a piece of Nordic history of New Testament scholarship in presenting three influential New Testament professors who were active during the first half of this century.

Lars Hartman, Birger Olsson. Teologiska Institutionen, Uppsala Universitet, Box 1604, S-751 46 Uppsala.

Contents

Foreword

June 16–19, 1986 a conference was held in Uppsala, Sweden, with approximately 60 participants from the Nordic countries of Denmark, Finland, Iceland, Norway and Sweden. They all belonged to the scholary field of New Testament Exegesis and represented different stages in training, experience and academic status. The work of the conference centered around problems of the Johannine literature and had the formate of lectures and seminars.

The discussions in the main papers and seminars revealed, not unexpectedly, a variety of perspectivs and approaches, which reflects the situation in the scholarly exegetical world at large. From the present publication of these main papers colleagues in the international scholary community will be able to sense something of this diversity. Thus, there is nothing like a Nordic (or Scandinavian – if we use that term to refer to the common linguistic basis) New Testament school. On the other hand, it is not difficult to find a certain tendency among the contributors to this volume to adopt some sort of a textcentered, text-as-literature, or reader-orientated approach, although no claims for methodological monopoly are raised. The tendency mentioned can be observed in spite of the differences in terms of method and topic in the contributions of Pilgaard, Karlsen Seim, Kieffer and Hartman. Such approaches do not exclude historical questions, and thus the papers by Sandelin and Olsson are no alien phenomena in the context.

Riesenfeld's presentation of three influential New Testament professors of an earlier generation demonstrates that it is not a new trend in the Nordic countries for New Testament scholars to combine a variety of approaches with common interests and mutual friendship. Actually it is part of our heritage.

Lars Hartman   *Birger Olsson*

The Johannine Writings within the Setting of Their Cultural History

Karl-Gustav Sandelin

The first part of this paper was originally written only for the conference at Uppsala, and, in fact, without thought of its publication. I have taken the liberty of tuning down some of the features which, upon reflection, may have been exaggerations on my part, i.e. the discussion that followed my presentation of the paper has left its mark on the present text. The second part is basically chapter 8 of my book *Wisdom as Nourisher* published some months after the conference as Vol. 64, no. 3 in the series Acta Academiae Aboensis, Ser. A, Åbo 1986. In the present version I have dropped a large part of the discussion to be found in the notes of my book.[1]

I

Language and style

I think it is reasonable to subscribe to the judgement of Schnackenburg concerning the language of the Gospel of John: it reveals a semitic color, but also represents a quite correct, although not a very sophisticated Greek.[2] This indicates that the author moves within a cultural environment where Greek-speaking Jews formed an important element. This criterion does not carry us very far, however, when we try to determine the geographical environment of the Johannine writings.

Some features in the composition may take us further. My teacher Rafael Gyllenberg thought he had detected compositional elements which he labelled as *cyclic* in the Gospel of John.[3] As for myself, I find that the Gospel bears witness to stylistic awareness, feeling for composition and literary talent.[4] This in turn would indicate that there existed an individual, whom we may with confidence call the *author* of the Gospel of John, at a particular – and possibly fairly late – stage of its development into its present form.[5] This author must have had some erudition and was, presumably, a representative of a literary tradition. One might

[1] Here referred to as: Sandelin, Wisdom.

[2] R. Schnackenburg, *Das Johannesevangelium* (Freiburg, 1965) I, 94.

[3] R. Gyllenberg, "Cykliska element i Johannesevangeliets uppbyggnad", *Teologinen Aikakauskirja/Teologisk Tidskrift* 65 (1960) 309–315.

[4] Cf. M. Girard, "L'unité de composition de Jean 6, au regard de l'analyse structurelle", *Église et theologie* 13 (1982) 79–110.

[5] Cf. L. Schenke, "Die formale und gedankliche Struktur von Joh. 6, 26–58", *BZ* 21 (1980) 38.

combine this conclusion with the observations which Cazeaux has made recently concerning the composition-techniques in the writings of Philo.[6] This could indicate some links between the author of the Gospel of John and educated Jews in the diaspora.

The puzzling situation

Can we say anything of a more precise nature? The following statement of Käsemann is well known: "Wir tappen mehr oder minder alle im Dunkel, wenn wir über den historischen Hintergrund des Evangeliums Auskunft geben sollen, welche über das Detail hinaus das Ganze exakt bestimmt."[7] The question becomes even more complicated since we have to reckon with a pre-history of the Gospel of John, containing the formation of both oral and written units. If we reckon with the use of previous material by the author, this material must have its origin in some historical environment. Furthermore, one may have to reckon with different redactional phases preceding the decisive one in which the author was involved.[8] These phases must also have had their historical and cultural settings. In addition, the Johannine writings may reflect a fairly long and dramatic history of a specific religious group within early Christianity.[9]

Theoretically the different stages of the formation of the Gospel of John may have been influenced by different Jewish and non-Jewish religious groups. Scholars have seen features in the Gospel of John which point to Pharisaic, Essenian, diaspora-Jewish and Samaritan influences. The Gnosis-theory is also still alive among the attempts to determine the historical setting of the Johannine writings.[10]

Even if the task of saying something adequate about *the* historical and cultural setting of the Johannine writings may by far transcend my ability, I will make an attempt to present some viewpoints based on certain observations of my own. To begin with, I shall take up some features which I find typical of the Gospel of John in order to say something about the Gospel's environment. Later on I shall describe a more specific factor which I think exists in the idea-historical background of the Gospel, namely wisdom tradition. Traditionally the term "the

---

[6] J. Cazeaux, *La trame et la chaîne, ou les structures littéraires et l'Exégèse dans cinq des Traites de Philon d'Alexandrie* (Leiden, 1983) e.g. p. 65.

[7] E. Käseman, *Jesu letzter Wille nach Johannes 17* (Tübingen, 1967) 9f.

[8] See e.g. R.E. Brown, *The Gospel according to John* (I–XII) (Garden City, 1965) XXXIVff; M.-É. Boismard – A. Lamouille, *L'évangile de Jean.* Synopse des quatre évangiles en français. Tome III. (Paris, 1977).

[9] See the article by B. Olsson in the present volume.

[10] See J. Becker, "Das Johannesevangelium im Streit der Methoden (1980–1984)"; *TRu* 51 (1986) 56–65.

Johannine writings" signifies the Gospel, the Johannine letters and the Apocalypse. I shall here confine myself to the Gospel and the First Epistle of John.

Some typical features

According to the Gospel of John the Word (= the Son, the only begotten) "became flesh", i.e. the idea of incarnation is given a very precise formulation. At the same time, Jesus is nevertheless described in a way which makes him more or less super-human. Many of the colors in this portrait have their parallels in the Synoptics: nature wonders (Jn 2:7–9; 6:11–13, 19; cf. Mk 6), prescience and wondrous knowledge (Jn 1:48;2:25; 4:17–19 cf. Mk 2:8; Lk 7: 39, 47), an extraordinary ability to escape pursuers (Jn 7:30, 8:59; 10:39; cf. Lk 4:29f), healing of the sick at a distance (Jn 4:46ff, cf. Lk 7:1ff), raising of the dead (Jn 11; cf. Mk 5:35–42). But in the Gospel of John Jesus is even more supreme than in the Synoptics. This can especially be seen where Jn handles matters concerning the passion, death and resurrection of Jesus. At his arrest, those who are going to capture Jesus fall to the ground when he says: "I am he" (Jn 18:5f). There probably exists an allusion to the name of Jahwe here. In front of the High Priest, and especially before Pilate, Jesus in Jn behaves and speaks in a very sovereign manner. On the cross, Jesus says that he is thirsty (Jn 19:28). But he does so in order that the Scripture would be fulfilled. Not only the word of the Scripture, however, but also Jesus' own words uttered earlier in the Gospel, namely that the Son of Man would be lifted up like Moses lifted up the snake in the desert, become fulfilled at Golgatha (Jn 18:32). The noteworthy characteristic of the crucifixion scene in Jn is not that of hard suffering and being forsaken by God, so apparent in Mt and Mk. The event is more similar to the version of the Gospel of Luke. But when Jesus dies he does not even cry aloud according to Jn. Having stated that all was fulfilled, he just bowed his head and gave up (παρέδωκεν) his spirit. Here one may find a tone of triumph. As in the Synoptics, Jesus in Jn also predicts his resurrection. The feature particular to Jn, however, is that the implication of the words of Jesus is that he himself is going to raise his body (Jn 2:19–22). Taken together, the features presented above, give the impression that it is *Jesus* who is the producer of the drama in which he plays the principal part. In spite of the fact that Jesus shows human feelings (Jn 11:3ff; 12:27) and that his death appears to be understood as a real death and not merely an apparent one, I think it is correct to label the Christology of the Gospel of John as a "high" Christology. The divine aspect of Jesus is clearly more strongly accentuated than in the Synoptics.[11]

The Fourth Gospel strongly emphasizes the doctrine of creation and the idea that the world belongs to the Word, i.e. God himself (Jn 1:1–3, 11). Nevertheless, the world seems to be more the *stage* for the God who in Jesus reveals himself in it[12] than the *object* of God's redeeming activity. In the Gospel of John, it is true, Jesus states that God sent the Son into the world in order to save it, not to condemn it (3:17). But in reality the appearance of the Son in the world results in confrontation with it. The world repudiates God (see for instance Jn 8:30–59). The keynote is this: "... the world did not recognize him... his own did not receive him" (1:10f). It is the elect who believe in Jesus and who are saved (Jn 6:44–48; 10:26–29).

A similar tension between a universalistic programme and a very narrow carrying out of it I think is to be seen when we consider the ideas of reconciliation and forgiveness. Christ is the Lamb of God, who takes away the sin of the world (Jn 1:29), he dies for the people (11:51f), he lays down his life for the sheep (10:15), and when he is lifted up from the earth he will draw all men to himself (12:32). After his resurrection Jesus says to his disciples: "Receive the Holy Spirit. If you forgive anyone his sins they are forgiven." One would expect some episode in the Gospel of John where a sinner repents and is forgiven. But in the story of the Samaritan woman, for instance, nothing is said about forgiveness. The paralysed man at Bethesda is admonished but not forgiven (Jn 5:14). The man born blind (Jn 9) and whose eyes Jesus opens does not believe in Jesus because of a promise of forgiveness of his sins. He confesses his faith when Jesus reveals to him that he is the Son of Man (9:37f).

The virtual manifestation of sin according to the Gospel of John seems to be unbelief (8:31–47). The one who does not see who Jesus is remains in darkness (12:46–48). On the other hand, the man who comes into the light does this so that it may become evident that his deeds have been in accordance with the will of God (3:21). The following question is, therefore, appropriate: is the remission of sins necessary for such a man who has done the work of God, i.e. who believes in Jesus (6:29)? Is there in the Gospel of John any real connection between forgiveness and faith?

The washing of the disciple's feet by Jesus (Jn 13) can, to be sure, be seen as an act symbolizing forgiveness. But this does not appear unam-

[11] In my original paper I used the term "docetic", inspired by Käsemann's, *Jesu letzter Wille*, 51. But this brought about very strong opposition in the audience. I have chosen the term "high" Christology here. This term was suggested by H.C.C. Cavallin in one of the seminars during the conference at Uppsala.

[12] Käsemann, *op. cit.*, 28.

biguously from the text. The remission of sins seems to be more exception than rule. Peter is an exceptional instance. (Jn 18:15ff, 25ff; 21:15ff). But even in the case of Peter the forgiveness of his denial of Jesus can only be read between the lines. The Gospel of John does not give any hint that Peter was remorseful or unhappy when he heard the rooster. What is the meaning of this episode in Jn? Does it have any other function than to give one additional example of Jesus' ability to know things in advance? Not even the questions of Jesus to Peter in Ch. 21 result in a confession of sin. Instead we read how Peter confirms his love for Jesus, who, as Peter says, knows everything (21:17). It may be possible to see the thought of forgiveness implied here, especially if we ask for some aid from 1 Jn 3:19f. Here the readers, facing even the condemnation of their hearts, are encouraged to put their trust in God, "for God is greater than our hearts and he knows everything".[13] In any case, it is Jesus' exhortation to Peter to be a shepherd for the sheep that is in focus in Jn 21, not the thought that Peter becomes reinstated or forgiven.

I have the impression that the concept of reconciliation and forgiveness on the one hand is clearly expressed in the Gospel of John, but that, on the other hand, this idea has very small relevance for the world or for the believers/disciples who do not belong to the world. I think a commentary on Jn 3:16 is appropriate here. At least in Swedish tradition this verse is commonly seen as a summary of the idea of reconciliation. But, in fact, this idea has to be read into the verse. It says that God gave ($\overset{\text{'}}{\varepsilon}\delta\omega\varkappa\varepsilon\nu$, not: $\pi\alpha\rho\acute{\varepsilon}\delta\omega\varkappa\varepsilon$) his Son to the world. The verse talks of revelation, not of reconciliation. I doubt that there is more of reconciliation implied in $\overset{\text{'}}{\varepsilon}\delta\omega\varkappa\varepsilon\nu$ than in the word $\dot{\alpha}\pi\acute{\varepsilon}\sigma\tau\varepsilon\iota\lambda\varepsilon\nu$ in the following verse. In order to read Jn 3:16 in terms of reconciliation I think one has to have recourse to, for instance, 1 Jn 4:9–10. In a similar way, the thought of the remission of the sins of the believers has to be projected upon the Gospel of John from, for instance, 1 Jn 1:7–2:2. This is, perhaps, a sound procedure exegetically. The accents are, nevertheless, put differently in the Gospel and in the First Letter of John.

In the Gospel of John, Jesus admonishes those whom he has chosen to love each other (15:16f). He prays that they may be protected from evil (17:15). They are in the world, but they do not belong to the world (17:15f). The Gospel of John presupposes a Christian fellowship, but the concept of the "Church" is not clearly defined, nor that of the ministry of

[13] According to Boismard and Lamouille (see note 8) there exists a close redactional link between Jn 21 and a certain stratum of 1 Jn.

the Church.[14] Individual Christians have a fellowship with Christ – "I am the vine; you are the branches"– and with one another, indirectly through Christ and directly through mutual love. The world is the place where the friends of Christ should be active (15:14ff). Christ sends them into the world (17:18). In the world even others come to faith through their message (17:20). I presume that "the scattered children of God" (11:52) means all believers. Probably only these are meant in Jn 12:32, although Christ says: "When I am lifted up from the earth, I will draw all men to myself". The goal for the friends of Christ is precisely the place where he himself will go when he is lifted up (14:3; 3:13–15). Like a shepherd Christ leads his flock through an evil and hostile world to another world where his Father lives.

In the same way as Christian fellowship and Christian shepherds like Peter are presupposed in the Gospel of John, also sacraments like Baptism (3:5) and the Holy Communion (6:51ff) seem to be presupposed. But it is the Spirit which is important in both cases (3:6–8, 6:63). It is not actual bread and water which are stressed, but Christ himself, his word and his Spirit.

Conclusions

In summing up we might say that both the Christology and the ecclesiology of the Gospel of John are characterized by *distance* to the world. Christ is a foreigner to the world, the Christians are not of the world. Sin, especially if we confine us to the Gospel, is peripheral in the life of the disciples. In contrast to this distance there exist in the Gospel ideas which express a very close relationship between the divine sphere and the world. The latter is created through the Word of God, who loves it and who sends the same Word, his Son, to be its reconciler.

The Christian group forming the primary environment of the Gospel of John seems to be a bearer of early Christian tradition which contains ideas like those of creation, incarnation, reconciliation, remission of sins, Christian community and sacraments; all these ideas are to be found in the letters of Paul. At the same time, the attitude towards these concepts seems to be ambiguous in a strange way. The concepts are not, so to say, allowed to exercise their full effect.

What has been said may indicate that the Christian community behind the Gospel of John is one which has distanced itself not only from the world proper, but also from other early Christian groups. Whether we want to call such a group "sectarian", "pietistic", "isolationist" or

[14] See H.-J., Klauck, "Gemeinde ohne Amt? Erfahrungen mit der Kirche in den johanneischen Schriften", *BZ* 29 (1985) 193ff, 218–220.

something else is, I think, to a large extent a question of taste.

In any case the Gospel of John has been accepted by the main stream of the Christian movement. The tensions between the Gospel and the First Letter of John may point to a need to correct certain tendencies within the Gospel which were felt to be one-sided.

II

I said above that the Gospel of John may have been influenced by different Jewish traditions. In this second part of my paper I will concentrate upon the relationship between the Gospel of John and Jewish wisdom tradition.

In the Gospel of John, Christ speaks of himself as the one who offers living water (Jn 4:10, cf. Jn 7:37), the one who gives food that endures to eternal life (Jn 6:27) and the one who is the bread of life that comes down from heaven (Jn 6:33–35). Scholars, understandably enough, have seen a link between these utterances and the idea of Wisdom as nourisher. Among them A. Feuillet,[15] P. Borgen[16] and R. Schnackenburg[17] should be especially mentioned.

Under the headings below, I first discuss the similarities and differences between the Johannine account and the idea of Wisdom as nourisher as it is attested in Old Testament and Jewish tradition. I then proceed to ask on what grounds we may postulate that the idea of Wisdom as nourisher lies behind some of the ideas in the Gospel of John. I go on to explain that if we have reason to think that the idea of Wisdom as nourisher has had an impact on the Gospel, then it is also necessary to determine how that idea has been used.

Jesus as giver of living water

In Jn 4, where Jesus meets the Samaritan woman at the well of Jacob, verses 10–15 indicate a difference between two kinds of water. He who drinks of the water from the well of Jacob will be thirsty again, in contrast to him who drinks the living water which Jesus gives and which will become in him a spring of water welling up to eternal life. The background to the expression "living water" used by Jesus is the Old Testament idea of "living", i.e. running water, or fresh water from wells (Gn 26:19: φρέαρ ὕδατος ζῶντος). The text of Jn 4 assumes that the well of

[15] A. Feuillet, *Études Johanniques* (Paris, 1962) 72–83.
[16] P. Borgen, *Bread from Heaven*. An Exegetical Study of the Concept of Manna in the Gospel of John and in the Writings of Philo (Leiden, 1965) 154–158.
[17] R. Schnackenburg, *Comm.*, I, 465f. II, 58f, 214.

Jacob contains ordinary fresh water (v. 11). The water that Jesus has to offer is a different kind of "living water" from that which is to be found in the well of Jacob.[18] But the text does not state explicitly what the living water *is* that Jesus offers. It could be his words (cf. Jn 6:68) or the Spirit (cf. Jn 7:39) or it could mean the gift of eternal life itself.

In the texts where Wisdom is presented as nourisher, we find in certain instances that she offers water to drink. In Sir 15:3, Wisdom is presented as a woman who gives the water of understanding to drink to the one who fears God. Unlike Jesus in Jn 4:14, Wisdom in Sir 24:21 states that those who drink her will thirst for more. In the light of the similarity of the wording of Jn 4:14, and especially Jn 6:35, to Sir 24:21, it seems possible that the author of the Gospel is making a deliberate reference to Sir 24. If this is so, a contrast between the water given by Jesus and the drink which in the Book of Sirach Wisdom is said to be or give may well be implied. At this stage, however, we can only say that in Jn 4 there is an explicit contrast between "natural" and "supernatural" water.

In Philo's writings Wisdom is presented as a spring whose water is interpreted as instruction (Post 138, Ebr 112, Fug 195). The instruction given by Wisdom is imperishable (Det 115) and gives immortality to the soul (Post 122f). In LA III 161, Philo explains the difference between heavenly and earthly nourishment, although he there speaks of bread, not water. One cannot deny that there exists a resemblance between Wisdom offering water in Philo and Jesus offering water in Jn, and it is possible that the authors may be developing similar traditions for their respective purposes, but it is hard to imagine that the Gospel of John derives in any literal sense from Philo.

In Jn 7:37 Jesus says: "If anyone is thirsty, let him come to me and drink. . ." It is probable that here too Jesus is offering "living" water (cf. 4:14) although the words that follow speak in a somewhat obscure manner of "streams of living water" that "will flow from within" the one who believes. This living water is interpreted as the Spirit in v. 39. When Jesus in Jn 7:37 summons his hearers to come and drink, his call is very similar to the call of Wisdom in Pr 9:5 and Sir 24:19. The words ἐρχέσθω πρός με καὶ πινέτω (Jn 7:37) are very reminiscent of the expressions ἐκκλινάτω πρός με and ἔλθατε φάγετε τῶν ἐμῶν ἄρτων καὶ πίετε οἶνον in Pr 9:4f and the words προσέλθετε πρός με in Sir 24:19.

We may say, therefore, that the presentation of Jesus as offering "living water" in the Gospel of John has clear affinities with descriptions of Wisdom offering her drink in Old Testament and Jewish Wisdom

---

[18] R. Bultmann, *Das Evangelium des Johannes* (Göttingen, 1941) 132.

tradition. It must be noted, however, that not only Wisdom but also the Lord himself in the OT and in Judaism is described as one who gives water to drink. It is therefore reasonable to ask whether it is necessary to see Wisdom as nourisher as a model for Jesus offering "living water" in the Gospel of John.

According to Jr 2:13 the Lord says:

> My people have committed two sins:
> They have forsaken me,
> the spring of living water (πηγὴν ὕδατος ζωῆς)
> and have dug their own cisterns (λάκκους),
> cisterns that cannot hold water.

The contrast here is not the same as that in the mind of Jesus in Jn, i.e. between ordinary fresh water and water giving eternal life. The image is that of a spring giving a flow of water, contrasted with cisterns which have to be filled from outside, but which, in this case, cannot even hold water.

Jr 2:13 is the last verse of the passage 2:4–13. In it the Lord is spoken of as the spring of fresh water, whom the Israelites have abandoned for idols. These are in turn compared to bad cisterns. The thought in this verse resembles the statement in Ps 36:10 where God is addressed with the words "for with you is the fountain of life". The fact that LXX renders *meqôr mayim chayyîm* ("the spring of the water of life") in Jr 2:13 as πηγὴν ὑδατος ζωῆς ("the spring of living water") shows that the translator understood the water given by God as water which gives life. Precisely such an understanding is absolutely clear in Philo. Now in Fug 198f, Philo cites Jr 2:13 and says:

> "But I bow in awe when I hear that this spring is one of Life: for God alone is the Cause of soul and life, and preeminently of the rational soul, and of the Life that is united with wisdom (φρόνησις). For matter (ὕλη) is a dead thing, but God is something more than Life, an ever-flowing Spring of living (πηγὴ τοῦ ζῆν), as He Himself says. But the impious flee from Him, persist in leaving untasted the water of immortality (ἄγευστοι τοῦ τῆς ἀθανασίας ποτοῦ διατελέσαντες), and dig in their madness for themselves but not for God, putting their own works above the celestial gifts of heaven. . ." (198f).

God is the spring of life here and the water he gives is the water of immortality. This water is not contrasted with ordinary water, but there is a polarity in this text between the divine life of the soul and dead matter, evidence of Philo's anthropological dualism. Although there is no such dualism in the Gospel of John, there is surely a resemblance between this Philonic passage and Jn 4:13f. Philo contrasts soul and matter, the former having its source in God. Jn contrasts natural fresh water with water that gives eternal life and which is offered by the Son of God.

When the Gospel of John presents Jesus as one who offers living water, this may indicate that the author wants to describe him as the Lord rather than Wisdom (cf. also Is 49:10).[19] Support for this view may also be adduced from the fact that when Jesus, in Jn 7:37, invites people to drink of the water he gives, this does not only resemble similar invitations of Wisdom, but also that made by the Lord, who in Is 55:1 says: "Come, all you who are thirsty, come to the waters (οἱ διψῶντες, πορεύεσθε ἐφ' ὕδωρ)..."

Now it can of course be argued that when he describes Jesus as giving living water the author of the Gospel of John has *both* the Lord *and* Wisdom in mind. Does he think of Jesus as Wisdom incarnate? As Wisdom is the image of God's goodness (Wsd 7:26), so the Son reveals the Father (Jn 14:7, 9). In this connection it is surely important to take into account the fact that in the Gospel of John the Son has a much closer relationship to the Father than Wisdom has to God in any stratum of Jewish Wisdom tradition. So far as I know, Wisdom is never called "God" which is the case with the Word in Jn 1:1 and the only begotten in Jn 1:18.[20] The words of Jesus "I and the Father are one" (Jn 10:30) are not paralleled in any description of the relationship between Wisdom and the Lord. When Jesus, in Jn 4, is presented as one who like the Lord offers living water, this is in keeping with the description of the close relationship between the Father and the Son in the gospel as a whole (cf. Re 1:8; 7:17; 21:6; 22:1, 13, 17). The fact that Jesus is also described as Wisdom may notwithstanding have great significance. I shall return to this question later.

Christ as nourisher and nourishment in Jn 6

In Jn 6:27 two kinds of nourishment are contrasted, much as the two kinds of water are in Jn 4:13f. There is food which perishes and the food that endures to eternal life. The latter will be given by the Son of Man. Some verses later the theme of the manna in the desert is taken up (v. 31). According to the people this was the bread of heaven. Jesus however states that his Father gives the true bread from heaven. This bread of God comes down from heaven and gives life to the world (vv. 32–33, cf. vv. 38, 41). In v. 35 Jesus states that he is the bread of life (cf. vv. 48, 50, 51ab, 57). He also says that he who comes to him will never hunger and who believes in him will never thirst. Jesus says that he has been sent by the Father and is accomplishing his will (vv. 38–40, cf. vv. 44, 57).

---

[19] Cf. Feuillet, *op. cit.*, 66.
[20] Cf. C.K. Barrett, *The Gospel According to St. John.* An Introduction with Commentary and Notes on the Greek Text (2nd ed; London, 1978) 155f.

If we compare these statements with what we find in the descriptions of Wisdom as nourisher, we can observe several resemblances. The contrast between two kinds of food has a clear affinity with certain passages in Philo, for instance LA III 161f where we read:

> "... there are two things of which we consist, soul and body (ψυχή τε καὶ σῶμα). The body, then, has been formed out of earth, but the soul is of the upper air, a particle detached from the Deity: 'for God breathed into his face a breath of life, and man became a living soul' (Gn 2:7). It is in accordance with reason, therefore, that the body fashioned out of earth has food akin to it which earth yields, while the soul being a portion of an ethereal nature has on the contrary ethereal and divine food; for it is fed by knowledge (ἐπιστήμαις) in its various forms and not by meat and drink, of which the body stands in need.
>
> That the food of the soul is not earthly but heavenly (οὐράνιος), we shall find abundant evidence in the Sacred Word. 'Behold I rain upon you bread out of heaven...' (Ex 16:4). You see that the soul is fed not with things of earth that decay (γηίοις καὶ φθαρτοῖς), but with such words (λόγοις), as God shall have poured like rain out of that lofty and pure region of life (φύσις) to which the prophet has given the title of 'heaven'."

According to my interpretation Philo has the nourishment of Wisdom in mind here, since "heaven" often means the same as Wisdom in Philo's writings (eg. Agr 64f).[21] In the above passage, there is a polarity between earthly food which decays and the incorruptible food from heaven which runs parallel to the statements of Jesus in Jn 6:27, 32. In Philo, however, the idea of the two kinds of food is combined with his anthropological dualism, for which there is no analogy in John. It nevertheless seems possible to assert that the author of John's Gospel and Philo are probably drawing upon the same tradition, though in different ways.[22]

As is the case with Jn 4:13f and Jn 7:37, the verbal links between Jn 6:35, 37, 51ab and both Pr 9:1–6 and Sir 24 are also close. He who comes to Jesus receives the promise of life (cf. Pr 9:5f). Several scholars have pointed out that the expressions in Jn 6:35 and Sir 24:21 are particularly close,[23] but although the *words* are similar the essential meaning is different. In contrast to Wisdom, Jesus, as the bread of life, puts an end to hunger and thirst.

But it is not only similarity of expression that knits Jn 6 and Sir 24 together. In both passages, the one who offers nourishment is also presented as nourishment itself. In Sir 24:19, Wisdom offers her nourish-

[21] Sandelin, Wisdom, 89.
[22] Cf. Borgen, *op. cit.*, 170.
[23] *Schnackenburg, Comm.*, II, 59, Feuillet, *op. cit.*, 82f, Borgen, *op. cit.*, 155, Boismard-Lamouille, *op. cit.*, 197f.

ment and is at the same time an object of desire herself; and in v. 21 she talks of those who *eat her* (οἱ ἐσθίοντές με). In Jn 6:27, 51c Jesus says he will *give* nourishment, but in vv. 35, 48 (cf 51a) he calls himself the bread of life and in v. 57 speaks of the one who eats him (ὁ τρώγων με). In Philo we find that Wisdom, presented as a mother and a nourishing rock, is identified with the manna in Det 115–118. Here too there is no sharp dividing line between nourisher and nourishment. As a result of Philo's exegesis, Wisdom actually becomes the bread from heaven in that passage.

There has been much discussion by scholars about the origin of the expression "bread of life" (ἄρτος τῆς ζωῆς). In two studies R. Schnackenburg has reached the conclusion that the closest parallel is to be found in the romance Joseph and Aseneth,[24] where the Man from heaven calls the honeycomb which he offers to Aseneth "bread of life" (ἄρτος ζωῆς JosAs 16:16). In the context "life" clearly means immortality and incorruption. D. Sänger has argued that the meal in JosAs can be seen as a Wisdom meal.[25] But although the *bread of life* comes from heaven (JosAs 16:14), it is not identified with personified Wisdom, a figure who does not appear in the story. It is nevertheless remarkable that the closest parallel to the Johannine expression "bread of life" occurs in an early Jewish literary text which seems to bear witness to the theme of Wisdom as nourisher.[26]

When Jesus says that the bread of God comes down from heaven (καταβαίνων ἐκ τοῦ οὐρανοῦ Jn 6:33, cf. vv. 38, 41, 42, 50) reference is probably being made both to Jn 3:13 and to Nu 11:9 LXX (κατέβαινεν τὸ μάννα ἐπ' αὐτῆς, i.e. τῆς παρεμβολῆς). It should be noted, however, that the statements about the sending (πέμπειν, Jn 6:38f, 44) and descent of Jesus resemble similar statements concerning Wisdom in the Wisdom tradition. According to Sir 24, Wisdom first had her throne in heaven and then, in obedience to God's command, took her rest in Jerusalem (vv. 3–11). The idea of Wisdom being sent down from heaven is also found in Wsd 9, where "Solomon" beseeches God to send Wisdom from heaven to help him:

> Send her forth (ἐξαπόστειλον αὐτήν) out of the holy heavens
> And despatch her (πέμψον αὐτήν) from the throne of thy glory.
> That abiding with me she may toil,
> And that I may know what is pleasing before thee. (v. 10.)

---

[24] Schnackenburg, *Comm.*, II, 57f; "Das Brot des Lebens", *Tradition und Glaube* (Festgabe für K.G. Kuhn; ed. G. Jeremias a.o.; Göttingen, 1971) 335ff.

[25] D. Sänger, "Jüdisch-hellenistische Missionsliteratur und die Weisheit", *Kairos* 23 (1981), 232ff.

[26] See Sandelin, *Wisdom*, 151–157.

In Wsd 9:17 Wisdom is identified with the Spirit of God and in the following verse she is described as a saving power, a characteristic attributed to Jesus in Jn 6. Comparison could also be made between the descent of Jesus and the words of Philo in Gig 24 and 47, according to which the Spirit (=Wisdom) abides with the sages on earth.[27]

There are so many links between Jn 6 and texts describing Wisdom as nourisher, as well as other closely related texts, that it seems reasonable to conclude that the author of John's Gospel made use of the idea of Wisdom the nourisher as a model. Like Wisdom, Jesus is sent down from heaven and thereby accomplishes God's will; he has come down from heaven with a saving purpose; he gives life, and he is both a nourisher and nourishment itself. If the author of the Gospel of John has used the figure of Wisdom as nourisher as a model for Jesus in Jn 6, then it is probable that he has done so also in Jn 4:13f and 7:37. However, even though we may accept this speculation, it must be stressed that in Jn 6 Jesus is by no means just a copy of Wisdom. As we have already pointed out, in Jn the relationship between the Father and the Son is much closer than that between God and Wisdom. In Jn 6 we can observe many additional differences between Jesus and Wisdom.

In Jn 6:62 Jesus speaks of the Son of Man returning to heaven. It is true that in 1 En 42:1–3 Wisdom is described as a figure who looked for a resting place among men, but who returned to heaven because she did not find such a place; and there is undoubtedly a formal similarity between Wisdom and the Johannine Jesus at this point.[28] But as Schnackenburg[29] points out, the ascent of Jesus to heaven is seen in Jn as being part of his mission as redeemer (Jn 3:13f, cf 1:51). This is not the case with Wisdom in those texts which describe the type of "disappeared Wisdom".[30] Moreover, neither the idea of Jesus as the Word of God incarnate (Jn 1:14), which is also implied in Jn 6:42, 51c,[31] nor the references to the Eucharist in Jn 6:51c–58, have their roots in Wisdom tradition. The theme of Wisdom the nourisher occurs together with that

---

[27] Cf. Feuillet, *op. cit.*, 72ff.

[28] For the myth of the "ascending-descending redeemer" in early Judaism and Christianity see C.H. Talbert, *What is a Gospel? The Genre of the Canonical Gospels* (London, 1978) 57–77.

[29] Schnackenburg, *Comm.*, I, 442f.

[30] "Die entschwundene Weisheit", see H. Conzelmann, "Paulus und die Weisheit", *NTS* 12 (1965–66) 236.

[31] H. Weder, "Die Menschwerdung Gottes. Überlegungen zur Auslegungsproblematik des Johannesevangeliums am Beispiel von Joh. 6", *ZTK* 82 (1985) 356. Cf., however, Talbert, *op. cit.*, 58–61.

of the Eucharist already in Paul, in 1 Cor 10.[32] The theme of Wisdom as nourisher, as we find it in Jn 6 (where Jesus and not Wisdom is nourisher and nourishment), is, however, linked more intimately with the theme of the Eucharist than in 1 Cor 10.[33] The author of Jn certainly includes the theme of Wisdom as nourisher in his overall design. But that design also contains other important elements.

The author of the Gospel of John has used elements from the Wisdom tradition in a free and creative manner. He has had access to the concept of Wisdom sent from heaven as nourisher and nourishment (Sir 24). And he has combined this idea with the concept of the bread that has come down from heaven (Ex 16; Nu 11:9; cf. Philo in Det 115–118). Possibly he was also familiar with the expression ἄρτος ζωῆς from the Wisdom tradition (JosAs). But nowhere in that tradition does Wisdom say that she is the bread of life, although she often speaks in the first person (Pr 9:1–6; Sir 24). Out of elements from the tradition the author of the Gospel of John has created an impressive synthesis, crystallized in the words: "I am the bread of life. . . I am the bread that has come down from heaven."

Does this use of the theme of Wisdom as nourisher in the Gospel of John mean that the author sees the Son of God as being identical with Wisdom in early Jewish tradition?[34] Let us repeat the question we asked above: Is Jesus Wisdom incarnate according to Jn? I think it is unlikely. If the author of this Gospel had identified Jesus with Wisdom, would he surely not have made it plain by a direct statement? It should be noted that in Jn we also have the image of the vine used for Jesus (Ch. 15). This image is also applied to Wisdom in Sir 24. But it is to be observed that in Jn 15 nothing is said about the fruit of the vine being nourishment for believers. If the author of Jn had really wanted to identify Jesus with Wisdom, the way in which he uses the image of the vine is hardly what one would expect. The manner in which the image of the vine is developed is quite different from what we find in Sir 24. In Jn 15:5 we have "I am the vine, you are the branches". Thus, although there is a similarity between the Jesus of Jn and Wisdom, there is also an evident discrepancy between the two figures.

I even think it is possible to go one step further in trying to determine how precisely the Gospel of John actually makes use of the theme of

---

[32] Sandelin, Wisdom, 161f, 165ff.
[33] Sandelin, Wisdom, 167–172.
[34] Boismard and Lamouille, op. cit., 198, give an affirmative answer.

Wisdom as nourisher. To demonstrate this, I take as my point of departure an analysis of Jn 6:35 where Jesus says:

ἐγώ εἰμι ὁ ἄρτος τῆς ζωῆς
ὁ ἐρχόμενος πρός με οὐ μὴ πεινάσῃ.
καὶ ὁ πιστεύων εἰς ἐμὲ οὐ μὴ διψήσει πώποτε.

I am the bread of life.
He who comes to me will never go hungry,
and he who believes in me will never be thirsty.

We have already postulated a relationship between this affirmation (cf. Jn 4:13f) and the words in Sir 24:21, where Wisdom says:

οἱ ἐσθίοντές με ἔτι πεινάσουσιν.
καὶ οἱ πίνοντές με ἔτι διψήσουσιν.

Those who eat me shall still hunger and those who drink me shall still thirst.

Opinions differ as to whether in Jn 6:35 and 4:14 the author of the Gospel wants to distance himself from the idea expressed in Sir 24:21[35] or whether his thought is in fact in accord with that verse in Sir.[36] Let us consider whether it is necessary to choose between these two options.

When Jesus says that those who believe in him will never be thirsty, he expresses an idea similar to that in Jn 4:13f where he states that all who drink of the ordinary water of the well of Jacob will be thirsty again, whereas he who drinks of the water given by Jesus will never thirst and will have eternal life. The contrast is here between ordinary water and the *living* water given by Jesus. In Jn 6 there is a similar contrast between bread which nourishes the body and the true bread from heaven. The manna in the desert was of the former kind (vv. 26, 49), but Jesus himself and the bread he offers are of the latter kind (vv. 27, 32, 48–50). The first kind of bread perishes, and those who eat it will finally die, whereas the bread that Jesus both is and gives, brings eternal life.

It can therefore be maintained that it is not the contrast between the nourishment of Wisdom in Sir 24:21 and the nourishment of Jesus that is implied in Jn 4:13f; 6:35, but simply the contrast between natural and supernatural bread and water. Now Philo describes a related contrast in LA III 161f. Does the Gospel of John follow in principle the same line as Philo, i.e. that it is not earthly but heavenly nourishment that really

[35] J. H. Bernard, *A Critical and Exegetical Commentary on the Gospel according to St. John* (Edinburgh, 1928) 141; Borgen, *op. cit.*, 155; Schnackenburg, *Comm.* I, 465; Barrett, *Comm.*, 234; Weder, *op. cit.*, 340.
[36] Bultmann, *Comm.*, 136f; Feuillet, *op. cit.*, 83; Brown, *Comm.*, 269.

matters? Because of a different anthropology, heavenly nourishment is understood somewhat differently, but the structure of thought may be considered similar. For Philo heavenly nourishment is the teaching of Wisdom (even Wisdom herself, Det 115–118), in reality the Law, whereas according to Jn 6 it consists of Jesus himself (vv. 35, 48, 51 ab), his Eucharistic gifts (v. 51 cff.) and his word (v. 68).

This picture is, however, incomplete, because in Jn 6 there appears to be a contrast not only between natural and supernatural bread, but also a contrast between the bread that Jesus both is and gives and the bread that, according to the people, Moses had given their fathers (vv. 31–35).

The people in Jn 6:31 demand a sign from Jesus and refer to the Old Testament with the words: "He gave them bread from heaven to eat." The sentence is not a direct citation of any OT passage and may be seen as conflating Ex 16:4, 15 and Ps 78:24. The sentence is, moreover, strangely ambiguous. Who is the subject? In the OT passages alluded to, the words clearly have God as the subject. But in his reply in v. 32, Jesus, with great emphasis (ἀμὴν ἀμὴν λέγω ὑμῖν), says: "It is not *Moses* who has given *you* the bread from heaven. . ." as if the people had maintained that it *was* Moses who had given them bread from heaven. The dialogue becomes understandable, however, if the words of Scripture cited by the people are understood by the author of Jn in such a way that the denial of Jesus is a natural response.

This would be the case if the words "he gave them bread from heaven to eat" are taken to mean that *Moses* gave the fathers *and* their descendants bread from heaven. But how can the people maintain that Moses has also given *them* bread from heaven? One answer might be that what befell the generation of the desert has also befallen the Israel of the present (Mishnah, Pes X 5bc). But there remains a further possibility, namely that the bread from heaven given by *Moses* signifies the *Law*,[37] which is a possession of the Jewish people at present (Jn 7:19, 51; 10:34; 15:25, 19:7). Such an understanding of the heavenly nourishment is typical at least of the teaching of Philo, according to whom the manna is the word of God, identical with the Law of Moses. Every Sabbath this bread of heaven was offered in the synagogues (cf. Jn 6:59), where Wisdom was present as a figure providing nourishment (Mut 258ff). That the manna was understood as the Law is also attested in Rabbinic sources (Mek Ex 13:17).[38]

---

[37] Cf. Brown, *Comm.*, 262; Barrett, *Comm.*, 289f.
[38] See H. Odeberg, *The Fourth Gospel*. Interpreted in its Relation to Contemporaneous Religious Currents in Palestine and the Hellenistic-Oriental World (Uppsala, 1929) 243.

In any case, if the bread from heaven in Jn 6:31 is understood as the Law, both the reference to Moses and the change from the pronoun αὐτοῖς (v. 31) to ὑμῖν in v. 32 become understandable. By denying that Moses gave the people bread from heaven, Jesus in fact denies that Moses has given them the *true* bread from heaven in giving them the Law. Jesus himself is the true bread that has come down from heaven (vv. 32–35). To interpret the passage in this way is in keeping with the statement in Jn 1:17, according to which the Law was given through Moses (διὰ Μωϋσέως ἐδόθη) whereas Grace and Truth came through Jesus Christ.

To see the "bread from heaven" in Jn 6:31 as the Law does not preclude reference to the actual manna of the desert, given by God. The sentence "he gave them bread from heaven to eat" can have a double meaning. Dialogue in which the utterances can be understood in different ways is indeed typical of the Gospel of John (see Jn 3:3–5; 4:10–15; 6:34; 8:21–22, 31–35). In Jn 6, the true bread from heaven, Jesus himself, is contrasted with three kinds of bread that cannot give eternal life: the bread that was used in feeding the five thousand (v. 26f), the manna (vv. 31, 49, 58) and the Law (v. 31).

If the foregoing interpretation is correct, then it also sheds new light on Jn 4:13f and 6:35, in which there also appears to be a double meaning. The nourishment and the drink that Jesus offers are different in their effects, not only from natural food and drink, but also from the kind of nourishment offered by Wisdom in Sir 24:21, a passage alluded to in Jn 4:13f and 6:35. The nourishment given by Wisdom in the Book of Sirach is closely connected with the Law (Sir 15:1–3); he who is nourished by Wisdom never becomes satisfied (Sir 24:21). A similar thought can also be found in Philo (Som I 50). The pupil of Wisdom always wants to learn more. But according to Jn 6:35, he who has received the true bread from heaven (which the Law is not) receives ultimate satisfaction. The hunger which the true bread from heaven satisfies can scarcely be other than hunger for eternal life. This becomes clear when we see the relationship between v. 35 and v. 47. In the former it is stated that he who believes will never hunger and thirst; in the latter we are told that he who believes has eternal life. He who eats of the bread of life will live for all eternity (v. 50f). In Jn 6, Jesus maintains that he is the only one who can satisfy the hunger and thirst for eternal life. The words of Jn 6:35 do not in fact constitute any refutation of Sir 24:21. The author of Jn obviously alludes to the statement in that verse, but he does not take any direct stand with respect to what is said there, namely that it is impossible to have enough of the nourishment of Wisdom. It is clear that for the author of Jn the nourishment offered by Wisdom according to Sir 24:21 cannot satisfy hunger and thirst for eternal life. In the Gospel of John, Jesus as nourisher and bread of life does not incarnate the Wisdom of early Judaism but supersedes her. It is not Wisdom, but the Son of Man, who gives nourishment that endures to eternal life. In the Gospel of John the resemblance between Jesus and Wisdom as nourisher has the effective purpose of supplanting the latter.

Conclusions

If my observations concerning the impact of the theme of Wisdom as nourisher on the Gospel of John are correct, they confirm, I think, the idea that diaspora Judaism has been an active element in the historical setting of that Gospel. At the same time we can detect a dissociation from the Jewish heritage. Wisdom and the Law are belittled. Similar tendencies are to be found in gnosticism, although the dualism is much more radical there than in the Gospel of John.

The History of the Johannine Movement

Birger Olsson

The subject of my paper is not one of my own choosing. The sources we have are very fragmentary and difficult to handle. And earlier historical reconstructions do not produce any stronger conviction in the minds of those who want to follow in their steps. Raymond E Brown, writing on this subject, said some years ago: "If sixty percent of my detective work is accepted, I shall be happy indeed."[1] I dare not set any such percentage for what follows. My paper is very much like a freehand drawing where the lines are formed without one really knowing why. The reasons are very often not given. My sketchy presentation of Johannine Christians should primarily be regarded as a general result of some years of work on Johannine writings.

1. *Unique writings – a unique history*

Let me begin by quoting Augustine from his Homilies on the Gospel of John:

> There are two states of life... that are known to the Church, whereof the one is in faith, the other in sight;
> one in the temporal sojourn in a foreign land, the other in the eternity of the (heavenly) abode;
> one in labor, the other in repose;
> one on the way, the other in the fatherland;
> one in active work, the other in the wages of contemplation;
> one declines from evil and makes for good, the other has no evil to decline from and has great good to enjoy;
> the one fights with a foe, the other reigns without a foe;...
> the one is anxious with the care of conquering, the other secure in the peace of victory;...
> the one discerneth both good and evil, the other has only that which is good presented to view;
> therefore the one is good, but miserable as yet, the other, better and blessed.
> This one was signified by the Apostle Peter, that other by John.[2]

The Johannine writings are unique. This insight is very old and not in need in this context of any motivation or exemplification: Johannine Christology, Johannine eschatology, Johannine dualism, Johannine concepts such as σημεῖον, παράκλητος, μαρτυρεῖν, πιστεύειν εἰς,

---

[1] R.E. Brown, *The Community of the Beloved Disciple* (London, 1979) 7.

[2] Tractatus 124, quoted from *A Select Library of the Nicene and Post-Nicene Fathers of the Christian Church*, Vol. VII (ed. P. Schaff; Grand Rapids, 1974, repr.) 450.

γινώσκειν, the dramatic presentations, the dialogues, the discourses, etc. The Gospel of John and the three Epistles have their own character and there is every reason to look for a specific historical situation behind these writings, or several situations, since they are witnesses of at least two generations of Christians.

Even if you give place to a main narrator, or to several authors/ redactors, in the Johannine text-production, there is at the same time an important group of people, men and women, who are in a special way bound to the Johannine writings. The fates of these people are our main interest now in the first paper at this conference of Nordic New Testament scholars.[3]

One problem involves giving these people a proper name. The proposals are many: the Johannine Church, the Johannine Community, or Communities, the Johannine Group(s), the Johannine School, the Johannine Sect, or, quoting a scholar who describes Jn as a "Relikt einer in den Winkel abgedrängten urchristlichen Gemeinschaft". The Johannine group is "eine Konventikel mit gnostisierenden Tendenzen", "eine ecclesiola in ecclesia", "die ersten Zeugnisse christlicher Konventikelbildung".[4] These people could name themselves as "brethren", "friends", or "the elect lady and her children".

I have chosen a rather vague and broad concept in the title of my paper, the Johannine movement. The closest parallel to this choice of name is the Essene movement as we know it through Philo, Josephus and the Qumran documents.[5] My perspective is primarily inner-Jewish. What the Johannine writings refer to is still in the 80's a movement within Judaism. And when it leaves a Jewish environment it has some difficulties in orienting itself within the Christian Church.

Ten years ago Robert Kysar summarized the Johannine research – limited to the Gospel of John – in six points.[6] I want to give them *in modified form* as a background for my general outline of the Johannine movement.

1. Jn is the result of *a long, complicated process.* There are traditions, oral or written, which are essentially independent of the synoptic material. The long process includes revisions, expansions, corrections,

---

[3] A text-oriented reading of the Johannine writings should also include historical reconstructions, if we want to take the pragmatic dimension seriously. Beginning with the history of the Johannine movement ought to be regarded as a part of our main task of interpreting the Johannine literature.

[4] E. Käsemann in his *Jesu letzter Wille nach Johannes 17* (3rd ed.; Tübingen, 1971).

[5] Cf. J. Murphy-O'Connor, "The Essenes in Palestine", *BA* 40 (1977) 100–124.

[6] R. Kysar, *The Fourth Evangelist and His Gospel* (Minneapolis, 1975) 267–276.

and comments, with many people and several historical situations involved. In spite of this the linguistic material – and here we can include the Epistles – is remarkably uniform, which indicates that there is also a clear continuation in this long process.

2. Jn is *a group product*, "a community's document". Its content very strongly depends on situations of a group and corresponds, to some degree, to changes affecting this group. Therefore, Jn may with good reasons be interpreted from a specific history.

3. Jn is a witness of *a syncretistic heterodox Jewish milieu* – if we can use such a word as heterodox about a part of Judaism at this time. Relevant parallel material to Jn has to be taken from several different sources. Hugo Odeberg, who worked on Jn here in Uppsala 60 years ago, was on the right track.[7]

4. Jn is very much *a result of "the dialogue between the church and the synagogue"*. With this formulation Kysar forgets that the Johannine people for a long time were *both* Jews *and* Christians. They regarded themselves as the true, genuine people of God. The background of the Gospel is much more a process within Judaism and not a Jewish-Christian dialogue. The Gospel is primarily written for these Johannine people in order to strenghten them in their Messiah-belief, and this also after that they had been expelled from the synagogues.

5. Jn demonstrates "an innovative and sophisticated mode of Christian thought, *radically Christocentric in all its expressions*". Kysar describes the author as "one of the first formative Christian thinkers,. . . responsible for a number of significant steps in Christian thought". All Johannine themes are interrelated and rooted in a Christology. Therefore, a multitude of motifs – the evangelist is also "the most perfect artist of his genre known to history" – are held together in a well-conceived framework.

6. Jn fully attests to the fact that "the Johannine community is *a distinctive form of early Christian life and thought*". This is a conclusion drawn from what has just been said: its own singular traditions, historical milieu, and mode of thinking.

Furthermore Jn has its own singular group of people. What does this Gospel say – and the three Epistles – about these people? I will begin with a general outline of the three main periods in the history of the

---

[7] See H. Riesenfeld's paper in this volume.

Johannine Christians[8] and after that I will analyse what especially 3 Jn and 2 Jn may say about the Johannine situation in the province of Asia at about 100 A.D. Many things speak in favour of a reconstruction of the Johannine history "in reverse", i.e. beginning with the situation around 100 A.D.

2 A general outline

Three traumatic experiences have in a special way formed the Johannine movement, three crises, or three σχίσματα, to use a recurrent word in John (7:43; 9:16; 10:19). These three basic experiences are connected to different geographical areas. "Emigrations" of different kinds are a well-known phenomenon among these Christians, from Jerusalem and Judea, from Palestine as a whole, from the land beyond the Jordan, and from Syria.

2.1 The first schisma, Jerusalem, about 40–70 A.D.

The Johannine movement has its roots in Palestine, especially in Judea and Jerusalem. From here comes the disciple of Jesus who formed the Johannine group during its most productive period, an eyewitness but not one of the twelve, "the disciple whom Jesus loved". Like John the Baptist he probably came form priestly circles. He "was known to the high priest" (Jn 18:15) and "his" Gospel is saturated with priestly, cultic categories: the image of Jesus, the emphasis on purifications, the big feasts, etc. The opponents of Jesus in Jn are to a great extent the high priests. The belief in Jesus as the Messiah meant to this disciple and the people around him a revival of the relation between God and his people, a renewed covenant as announced in Jer 31. This new fellowship with God resulted in a new view of the temple in Jerusalem and of the role of the Samaritans in the new situation. A conflict with those who were faithful to the temple in Jerusalem (and on Gerissim) was occasioned by this.

A radical criticism of the temple was nothing new in the history of the Jews. We can mention the Samaritan conflict, or the Essene conflict, both of them partly priestly conflicts, or Stephen in Acts 6–7. In the Johannine movement the conflict with the Jews who were faithful to the

---

[8] As general references for my Johannine history, see R.E. Brown, *op. cit.*, O. Cullmann, *Der johanneische Kreis* (Tübingen, 1975); and K. Wengst, *Bedrängte Gemeinde und verherrlichter Christus*. Der historische Ort des Johannesevangeliums als Schlüssel zu seiner Interpretation (Neukirchen-Vlyun, 1981).

temple signified an orientation away from Jerusalem. Some of the Johannine Christians may have left Jerusalem and Galileans and Samaritans became an important part of the Johannine group. Jesus was confessed as the King of *Israel*, Israel being taken as the true Israel, as the scattered children of God, now brought together as a result of Jesus' death. "When I am lifted up from the earth, I will draw all men to myself", Jesus says in Jn 12:32.

Their understanding of this Jesus during this period became increasingly stamped by ideas related to Moses – Jesus as the Prophet, the great Revealer – something that was promoted by covenantal thinking and a connection with Samaritans.

This was the first serious *schisma* in the Johannine movement. At the latest these people left Jerusalem during the disturbances in Judea in the 60's. They probably left Palestine as a whole and emigrated eastward to areas beyond the Jordan. Many Jews had already lived there before this, as well as Samaritan families who had returned from Babel. Intercourse with Jews was still an important part of their identity and self-understanding, in spite of sharp conflict with Jewish groups.

2.2 *The second schisma, beyond the Jordan, about 70–90 A.D.*

In the beginning of the 50's King Agrippa II obtained the areas east of Jordan that once belonged to the tetrarch Philip. In his politics he was both faithful to Rome and generous to the Jews. Many Christians found a homeland in his territory after 70 A.D., including Johannine Christians who were probably scattered in small groups, "Johannine houses", with a centre where the Beloved disciple and other teachers and tradents were located, the so called Johannine school. Itinerant apostles and profets – of the same type as those in the Didache – played an important role in connecting these different groups.

Two changes, however, strongly influenced the Johannine movement during these two decades: a continued development of the group's confession of Christ and an initial removal of people with dissonant opinions from the Jewish communities. Jn manifests a movement towards a "high" Christology in which Jesus' divinity and pre-existence were stressed. As a result, Jews could accuse Johannine Christians of making Jesus a god beside God. At the same time, they began to read curses in the synagogue services against "heretics" (*minim*). This liturgical curse also included the Johannine Christians.

This episode of antagonism resulted in a divorce in the 80's, *schisma* number two. The Johannine Christians were put out of the synagogues and thereby lost their inherited social setting. "The Jews" were henceforth regarded as the children of the Devil.

The view of Jesus as being the answer of God's promises to the Jewish people was strengthened in this situation, with a stronger presential eschatology as a result. Jesus and what had come with him replaced all the Jewish heritage they lost when they were expelled from the synagogues.

The Jewish leaders in Jamnia seemed to have had good relations with the administration in the King Agrippa's kingdom so that the clean-up in the synagogues was effective. This had a double effect: the Johannine group became more open to non-Jewish people and they had to make a move again, this time to the west.

2.3 *The third schisma, Asia Minor, about 90–110 A.D.*

The expulsion from the synagogues and the movement westwards reinforced the universalistic possibilities in Johannine thinking, i.e. Jesus as the Saviour of the world. Furthermore, many "Greeks" seemed to have joined the Johannine movement. In the 90's several small Johannine communities appear in the province of Asia. As in earlier times, itinerant brethren had an important role in holding together the different groups and the unity and the solidarity among them became emphasized.

The reaction to the Johannine mission, however, was very often negative. Some did not accept the message, others persecuted the Johannine Christians. Jewish-Christians had difficulties with their high Christology. And contacts with other Christians were not without problems.

It is in this more open situation that the Johannine movement was broken up. The losts of a Jewish setting surely contributed to this tragedy in the Johannine history, as also did the addition of new members to the group. A strong one-sidedness and imbalance in the Johannine Christology, however, may have been the most important background to this division.

According to 1 Jn a group had split the Johannine fellowship. "They went out from us", 1 Jn 2:19. These secessionists did not fully accept Jesus' humanity. His earthly work had no saving significance to them. Everything depended on the knowledge ($\gamma\nu\tilde{\omega}\sigma\iota\varsigma$) Jesus had brought to them. Those having this knowledge of God were already saved here and now.

The group that remained around the Presbyter – the man behind 1–3 Jn – acknowledged that Jesus Christ had come in the flesh ($\dot{\epsilon}\nu\ \sigma\alpha\rho\varkappa\dot{\iota}$), and stood steadfast by the tradition from the earthly Jesus as transmitted by the Johannine school (or a part of it). The Spirit and the tradition, both of them witnessed to the truth. The earlier opposition between Johannine Christians and Jews was linguistically transformed in this situation to parties within the Johannine movement. The secessionists are described as the children of the Devil, and so on.

According to Raymond E. Brown,[9] the more tradition-faithful part of the movement joined other Christian communities at the end of this period. The Johannine Christians recognized other traditions without giving up their own. The secessionists seemed to have lost contact with the church and became a part of the Gnostic movements.

3. Situation in the province of Asia about 100 A.D.

A reconstruction of the history of the Johannine movement should begin "in reverse", i.e. in Asia Minor about 100 A.D. We have the best sources for this period and the two smallest Epistles are historically the most concrete of all the Johannine writings.

In one of the latest articles on the subject, "Die Anfänge der johanneischen Schule", published in New Testament Studies at the beginning of this year,[10] Georg Strecker takes this starting point in the two short letters and maintains that these are original documents of the founder of the Johannine school. If not, they should never have become a part of the Christian canon. According to his reading, 2 Jn argues for a chiliastic doctrine: Jesus is to return.

This interpretation is very difficult to verify in the letter as a whole. I am not convinced by Strecker's main thesis but would agree with him that scholars neglect 2–3 Jn when they try to describe the Johannine movement. The second part of my paper is primarily dedicated to an evaluation of these letters.

What about the Book of Revelation as a source for a historical reconstruction of the Johannine movement, the only book in the New Testament that has a person named John as its author? I myself have become increasingly interested in connecting the Apocalypse with the Johannine writings, an impossible thought for most New Testament scholars.[11] There are some linguistic similarities, the structuring of the

---

[9] R. E. Brown, op. cit., 145ff.

[10] NTS 32 (1986) 31–47.

[11] E. Schüssler Fiorenza, "The Quest for the Johannine School: The Apocalypse and the Fourth Gospel", NTS 23 (1976–1977) 402–427, O. Böcher, "Johanneisches in der Apokalypse des Johannes", NTS 27 (1980–81) 310–321, S. S. Smalley, "Keeping up with Recent Studies. XII. St John's Gospel", Exp Tim 97 (1986) 106, and G. Kretschmar, Die Offenbarung des Johannes (Stuttgart, 1985) 24f.

material has common features, the Christology of the Apocalypse reminds of the Gospel of Jn (for example the motifs of sacrifice and victory), the same can be said about the prophetic structure of authority, both writings have their roots in Palestine, etc.

The Johannine movement, as I use the term in this paper, is not only the (orthodox) group behind 1 Jn but also persons and groups who may be more or less in a marginal area. The letters witness to different parties within the movement, and according to 1 Jn a large part of the movement has gone their own way. If we take this "secessionist group" as a left wing within the movement, characterized by an advanced Johannine development, it is not difficult to place the Book of Revelation at the extreme right. The Apocalypse of John may very well consist of such apocalyptic material that functioned within (a part of) the Johannine movement, especially in the earlier periods. At the end of the first century Johannine components are divided into different groups. 1 Jn has, for example, more Jewish apocalyptic material than Jn and the short letters have a peculiar mixture of profane Greek, Jewish-Christian and Johannine language. The Book of Revelation may be assigned a place within the movement, although not at its centre. In what follows I want to concentrate on the two short letters.

The temporal or logical order between the three Johannine letters is not given by their designations. The traditional order comes from volume and importance and from closeness to 1 Jn. One can find almost all the possible orders among modern scholars: 1–2–3, 1–3–2, 2–3–1 and 3–2–1. The choice to a great extent depends on how one reconstructs the historical situation common to the Johannine writings about 100 A.D. In 1 Jn the serious crisis is solved by theological activity and teaching, in 2 Jn and 3 Jn by some practical procedures. According to my reading, the shorter letters reflect more an earlier stage than a later one in the Johannine development. The community situation behind them is not so static, whereas 1 Jn looks back on the tragic schism and assures its readers that they in their faithfulness to "that which was from the beginning" have eternal life to the full, 1 Jn 5:13; 2:12–14; 1:1–4. There are, perhaps, different locations behind the letters. Under all circumstances the three letters are close to each other in time and reflect related situations in the fall and decline of the Johannine movement.

3.1 *The witness of 3 Jn*

3 Jn is the most private letter in the New testament and at the same time the most profane in its use of traditional letter conventions. It is a recommendation for Demetrius and other itinerant brethren but does

not have the traditional form of a recommendation letter. The ordinary motifs (one's own particular position, glory, advantages) are missing.

3 Jn has its own rhetorical strategy.[12] It is impossible to evaluate the letter with regard to our subject without analysing it. I will do so in a very informal way, verse by verse, focusing on the dynamic interaction between S (sender) and R (receiver) in the document:

Vv. 1–2. S binds R to himself by a threefold use of ἀγάπη words. In Greek letters ἀγαπητός is seldom used for characterization, but other similar words are used instead. Both of them are φίλοι (cf. v. 15): S explicitly says so, R is supposed to be so. This basic relationship is expressed throughout the whole letter: vv. 1, 2, 5, 11, 15 (implicitly).

This ἀγάπη relation is furthermore qualified by the title ὁ πρεσβύτερος and the corresponding concept of τὰ ἐμὰ τέκνα in v. 4, and by the phrase ἐν ἀληθείᾳ, v. 1. R belongs to the children of the presbyter, they are both members of the Johannine community of love. The presbyter is the link with the beginning of the Johannine movement (the hander-on and interpreter), the one who is responsible for the true Johannine tradition, the ἀλήθεια.

With the addition of ἐν ἀληθείᾳ – not a common phrase in the Greek language – S has announced two main arguments for his case, ἀγάπη and ἀλήθεια. Both of them stress the unity, the fellowship and the solidarity of the Christian community. The word ἀλήθεια is also repeated later on in important parts of the argumentation, vv. 3, 4, 8 and 12.

V.2. Already in this introductory part the sender intimates in very general terms that R will do something that the sender requests: καθὼς εὐοδοῦταί σου ἡ ψυχή. It may be read as a statement from the sender's point of view (what should be proved by the acts of R is simply stated) but the phrase is open to some confirmation from R. The common wish of health is used as a general part of the argumentation.

V.3. The focus is changed from the more general σου ἡ ψυχή to the more specific σου τῇ ἀληθείᾳ but with the same kind of argumentation as in v.2. The sender states what is to be proved by the acts of the receiver. The witness is no longer only the sender, vv. 1–2, but brothers who come and go in the congregations involved in 3 John.

V.4. S implicitly exhorts R for the first time: You are my children when you walk in the truth. If you want to be my children, you have to continue to walk in the truth.

---

[12] See my article "Structural Analyses in Handbooks for Translators, *BT* 37 (1986) 117–127.

V.5. R already shows his faithfulness (πιστὸν ποιεῖς) in working for the itinerant brethren. Not only S (v.2) and the brethren (v.3) know this, but also the whole congregation (the congregation of the presbyter or the church as a whole; cf. a witness from all in v. 12). Σου ἡ ψυχή and σου ἡ ἀλήθεια is further specified by σου τῇ ἀγάπῃ in v.6.

V.6. An explicit petition, but a very modest and polite one: "Please, help them to continue their journey." The phrase is very much embedded, syntactically and argumentatively (with background material before and after it).

V.7. The request in v.6 is given a new motivation: a reference to their commitment to the Name, and to their relation to the "unfaithful".

V.8. The request of v.6 is repeated but in a rather implicit form with regard to R. "We" is used instead of "you" and there are no imperatives. You and I and persons like us (=Johannine Christians?) are obliged to help these people. Another argument is added: cooperation with the truth.

Vv.9–10 give further motivations by way of a negative example. Diotrephes, in his very negative attitude to the brethren, does not cooperate with the truth. His works are described more and more negatively in this part of the letter.

V.11 includes the only explicit imperative in 3 John, μὴ μιμοῦ. The formal structure of this verse (chiasm, repetitions), summarizing what has been said and adding the most crucial argument (to have fellowship with God or not), gives it a very heavy position in the argumentative structure. Its very general form is remarkable. The problem does not seem to be the attitude to one person alone (Demetrius). The strategy is clear: S wants R to draw his own conclusions with regard to the itinerant brethren.

V.12 may be read as the most distinct expression of the message of the letter: "We recommend Demetrius." At the same time it is a very indirect form of recommendation. Demetrius is given merely as an example. The main message is a modest but very strong appeal for R to continue the fellowship and to show solidarity with these itinerant brethren, who work for the truth. This is a very crucial relationship for S.

Vv.13–15 have primarily a terminal function but contribute also to the argumentation. They express the close relation between S and R and link up with the ἀγάπη motif and through this with the beginning of letter. Notes on the author's writing activity render importance to what is written. The letter and its message could not wait. So serious was the situation.

36

This small document gives us essential information about the situation in Asia Minor:

1. The Johannine fellowship consists of *several groups* located at a distance from each other: the presbyter and the friends with him, Gaius and his friends, the church as a whole in the place where Diotrephes and Gaius are. More than one Johannine Christian has a house large enough to provide accommodation for travelling brethren: Diotrephes, Gaius, other Christians in Diotrephes' community. This presupposes a certain economic status among some Johannine Christians. We may add that the persons in 3 Jn have typically Greco-Roman names: Gaius, Diotrephes, Demetrius.

I interpret the presbyter as the main person in the Johannine school of this time responsible for the Johannine tradition. Both Gaius and Diotrephes belong to the Johannine group, but the presbyter seems not to have met them personally. Is he still in the Syrian area?

3 Jn, therefore, witnesses to a Johannine centre (where the presbyter is) and to small house communities of Johannine character in the neighbourhood of each other.

2. There is *a disunity* within the Johannine movement at this time, within a fellowship that more than any other in the New Testament stresses mutual affinity and solidarity. The presbyter takes this very seriously, writes a diplomatic letter and relates the problem to fellowship with God or not. Diotrephes will not accept "us", i.e. those teachers and tradents who hold the Johannine movement together. He casts suspicion upon the authority of the presbyter through slander and shows his negative attitude by not welcoming travelling brethren.

3. *Travelling brethren* have a very important function in the situation of the letter, vv. 3, 5–8, 10,12. But who are these brethren?

The first answer should be: We know very little about them. The material is very limited and can be interpreted in different ways. At the same time a classification of these people is crucial for understanding 3 Jn and important for reconstructing Johannine history. So we will make an attempt.

In my opinion we have to choose between two alternatives:

1. Itinerant teachers (tradents, exegetes) within the Johannine community closely related to the presbyter. Raymond E. Brown calls them "the Presbyter's indispensable weapons against the spread of the secession", "the Presbyter's countermissionaries", "the anti-secessionist missionaries".[13]

[13] R. E. Brown, *The Epistles of John* (New York, 1982) 738, 742f, 746 and 750f.

2. Itinerant apostles and prophets in a broader sense, known to us through the Didache and other sources, working in the marginal area of the Johannine movement. Several observations speak in favour of this latter alternative.

a. There is not only a closeness between the presbyter and the brethren but also a marked distance, v.8, v.12. To the Johannine "friends" Gaius and Diotrephes they are strangers, v.5, v.9f, in need of recommendations.

b. In the Johannine phrase in v.8 there is a distance between "we" and "such men", giving "we" the primary meaning of "we Johannine Christians". The same applies to "we" and "Demetrius" in v.12.

c. These travelling people are always called "brethren", not the more Johannine "beloved", "friends" or "children".

d. The affinity to the truth is emphasized in v.8 and v.12. Truth is an important Johannine concept but can in the context of some (Jewish) Christian words in 3 Jn be given a broader sense: the truth as manifested in Jesus Christ and in those who follow him, in words and ways of life.[14]

These observations, and others, provide me with the hypothesis that the author of 3 Jn strongly argues for a continued fellowship with Jewish-Christian wandering preachers, probably of Syrian-Palestinian origin, in their way of living as true followers of Jesus and to some extent also as transmitters of Jesus traditions.[15] Like brother John in the Book of Revelation, they may have represented a more Jewish apocalyptic form of Christian tradition. Their role in the young church had some parallels with the author of 3 Jn: to secure the life-giving connection backwards to Jesus himself in words and deeds.

Very hypothetically the situation may be described in this way: The presbyter, like a part of the Johannine movement, is still in Syria. Some Johannine Christians have "emigrated" to Asia Minor with the formation of some new house communities as a result. To these belong Gaius' and Diotrephes' houses. In this new situation and in a continued inner-Johannine development the Johannine fellowship began to break down. The distance to the Jewish heritage increased, which was expressed, among others, in a negative attitude to Jewish-Christian travelling preachers. Through these people the presbyter got information about

---

[14] The intinerant prophets in the Didache "teach the truth", 11:10.

[15] See G. Kretschmar, "Zur Entwicklungsgeschichte des Wanderradikalismus im Traditionsbereich der Didache", *Wiener Studien* 11 (1977) 145–167 (with references), J. Roloff, "AMT/Ämter/Amtsverständnis", *TRE* Bd 2 (Berlin – New York, 1978) 515f, and D. Tidball, *An Introduction to the Sociology of the New Testament* (Exeter, 1983) 28ff, esp. 42–46 (with references).

the situation in different areas and he used to write recommendation letters for some of them to his "friends" in Asia Minor. When Diotrephes refused to welcome the brethren he wrote to Gaius: Continue to support them. The attitude to them is related to the truth, v.8. Not accepting them means in a broader perspective not accepting the presbyter and his collegues, which in turn means a departure from the truth revealed in Jesus Christ. Those who welcome these brethren are of God, those who do not have not seen God, v.11. Only a right connection with Jesus Christ, in words and deeds, secures fellowship with God.

Given this interpretation 3 Jn is written before the great schism referred to in 1 Jn. The following shorter analysis of 2 Jn gives us a similar result even if 2 Jn is much closer to 1 Jn. Is 2 Jn a letter to the Johannine Christians in Ephesus before the presbyter came to the city?

3.2 *The witness of 2 Jn*

2 Jn is very much bound to 3 Jn (letter formulas) and to 1 Jn (related themes) but has its own strategy. With regard to the argumentation the letter can be described in this way:

a. A basic starting point: the very close affinity between "all who know the truth", i.e. between Johannine Christians who still accept the tradition from Jesus Christ as transmitted by the Presbyter, "the teaching of Christ". The author uses many words from the family sphere πρεσβύτερος, κυρία, τέκνα, πατήρ, υἱός and in v.12 ἀδελφή and concepts which remind of a society of covenantal character: ἀγαπᾶν, γινώσκειν, μένειν ἐν, εἶναι μετά, ἐκλητός, χάρις, ἔλεος and εἰρήνη.

Sender and receiver are first and foremost knitted together by *truth* and *love*, words which are accumulated in the very enlarged opening of the letter (five and four times respectively). Union with God and Jesus Christ is expressed in v.9 with the very strong words "to have the Father and the Son", probably a covenantal phrase.[16] This basic fellowship (κοινωνία) between sender and receiver is reinforced by the two last verses of the letter: there is much more to talk about, the hope of a visit, a face-to-face talk, experience of a full, mutual joy, greetings from "the children of your chosen sister". This strong thematic framework (the very close covenantal fellowship) is quite fundamental to the other three parts of the letter.

---

[16] The very rare phrase is used about the people of God in 2 Clem 2:3. Israel in the Old Testament is the possession of God, Ex 19:5f.

b. A petition, mostly in we-form: Let us love one another. Truth and love, which so fully determine the status of both sender and receiver, have to find expression in acts, in their way of living. The author begins with some laudatory terms, v.4, and refers after that to what they have in common, to what they "have from the beginning", vv.4–5. This prepares for a rather polite request which first includes the author (we-form, v.5) and then is delimited in more general vocabulary to the addressee (you-form): you should walk in it (in the command).

c. A motivation for this request which the receiver quite likely had heard very often and regarded as natural and given. The new motivation is very clear: the serious risk that the fellowship breaks down, that they loose what they have worked for, what they are to receive in the fullness of time, vv.7–9. The danger was caused by travelling teachers who had lost contact with the teaching of Christ and thereby with God himself, v.9.

d. A specific exhortation: Do not welcome these teachers in your community, v.10. Anyone who welcomes them shares in their wicked and destructive work, v.11. The fellowship of truth and love on earth breaks down.

This well constructed letter verifies some of our earlier conclusions:

1. The Johannine fellowship consists of *several groups*, described in 2 Jn as "the elect lady and her children" and "the children of your elect sister". The Johannine Christians who have the teaching of Christ form a family of truth and love. The very strong emphasis on this covenantal fellowship in the opening of the letter is motivated by the risk of its further disintegration.

2. There is *a disunity* within the Johannine movement, in this case over Christology. Some have departed and not remained in the teaching that Christ has given them and the command they got from the Father. I read this information in vv.7–11 in connection with 1 Jn and interpret the "deceivers" as Johannine Christians who have deceded.

3. *Travelling teachers* are presupposed as a natural phenomenon within the Johannine movement. In 2 Jn they seem to be known by the community but not welcome any more. The presbyter gives us very little information about them. Perhaps he does not know so much about the situation. 1 Jn gives us more information.

3.3 *The witness of 1 Jn*

To describe the genre of 1 Jn is very difficult. The letter is in my opinion primarily an edited collection of the presbyter's teaching with regard to the serious and irrevocable schism that came upon the Johannine movement. The schism is regarded as a fact, belonging to the past. Any intercourse between the two parties did not exist any more. In various ways the author wanted to remove the insecurity of the "faithful", to assure them that they have eternal live, those who believe in the name of the Son of God, 1 Jn 5:13. The risk of apostasy is not quite eliminated as yet. Some scholars suppose that most Johannine Christians became secessionists and that these people had "the world's goods", 1 Jn 3:17, and belonged to those who were richer.

The presbyter's opinion of the schism – we find it expressed best in 1 Jn – is crucial for a reconstruction of the history of the Johannine movement. The very unique and peculiar component of the Johannine thought turned out to be its great weakness in a new situation. The Johannine schism is very much a result of an inner Johannine development. We can summarize it very simply under four points.[17]

3.3.1. *God on earth*

The experience of God's presence on earth was important for the first Christians. In his message of the kingdom of God Jesus seems to have stressed *both* something "already now" *and* something "not yet", a combination of presential and futural eschatology. This doubleness was represented within the Johannine movement from the beginning, but for many reasons one side became increasingly emphasized: God's presence here and now through Jesus Christ and his own. The loss of the temple, of the synagogue service, and of the Jewish framework may have contributed to this accent. Finally, some denied a futural component. The presbyter wanted to keep the double character, 1 Jn 2:28–3:3. "The darkness is passing away and the true light is already shining", 1 Jn 2:8, although he came very close to the secessionists' opinion, 1 Jn 3:9–14; 5:4–12.

3.3.2. *Jesus on earth*

Christology is the very centre of Johannine thought. With regard to the balance of Jesus' humanity and his divinity no early Christians have stressed Jesus as God so strongly as the Johannine group. This may be seen in the accent on his preexistence, his unity with the Father, his divine doxa. Both sides were confessed to among the Johannine Christians, but the secessionists seem to have cut off the one side, i.e. to have taken a further step in the direction of Jesus as God. Jesus' earthly work

[17] See R. E. Brown, *The Community* (see note 1) 109–144.

(his way of life, his teaching, his death) lost its significance for them. They did not confess that Jesus Christ has come in the flesh, 1 Jn 4:2f.

3.3.3. *The Spirit on earth*

1 Jn mentions the Spirit very seldom. Probably the presbyter and the secessionists were very close to each other in their opinion of the Spirit. The presbyter, however, stresses the tradition and binds the Spirit to what they heard from the beginning, 1 Jn 2:20–25. This may indicate that the secessionists referred to the teaching of the Spirit as God's direct words to those who know him – without Jesus and the tradition from him serving as a link between God and the Spirit.

3.3.4. *The disciples on earth*

Divine doxa marked out not only Jesus but also his disciples on earth. A dualism between the disciples and the world, between "we" and "they", gradually increased with some Johannine Christians, partly depending on traumatic experiences within the movement. The secessionists maintained that they had no sins. They could say: We are clean. Those who have bathed do not need to wash, Jn 13:10. On this point the presbyter has difficulties in his argumentation. He comes very close to his opponents. But he wants to maintain a form of "both/and", 1:5–2:2; 3:4ff.

The secessionists, therefore, although very closely related to the presbyter, had moved a step further. The presbyter regarded this difference not merely as an innocent imbalance in their opinion but as something quite crucial. These people do not "have God". Fellowship with God is a fellowship with Jesus Christ which is a fellowship with "us", i.e. with those who were responsible for the Jesus tradition within the Johannine movement.

4. *The situation before 100 A.D.*

My sketchy presentation above of the history of the Johannine movement depends a lot on works by R.E. Brown, O. Cullmann and K. Wengst.[18] I am not going to give you their arguments now or discuss them – mostly analyses of Jn. I only wish to add two possible sources for this period.

---

[18] See note 8.

4.1 *1 Jn as witness of the beginning*

The presbyter refers very often to what was from the beginning, i.e. the time when the addressee first met the Christian message. He gives information about earlier stages in the history of the movement. And those who read/heard his letter, among them some older men, are supposed to accept what he says. He needs not argue for his status or authority. If the presbyter is telling the truth, what information do we get about earlier stages? Not least, the covenantal setting "of the old days" ought to be explored for a historical reconstruction.

4.2 *Jn 1:19–4:54 as symptoms of the Johannine history*

The Gospel of John has three introductions: 1:1–18; 1:19–2:12; 1:19–4:54. This is a presentation of the beginning: the gathering of disciples, including Samaritans and Galileans; the replacement of Jewish purification, and of the temple (Jerusalem, Gerissim); different attitudes of the Jewish leaders; relations to John the Baptist, etc. If the point of view for editing this part of the Gospel is how a renewed people of God is born out of the old one,[19] what does it tell us about the beginning of the Johannine movement?

5. *A concluding remark*

The Johannine movement is not a homogenous phenomenon. Many scholars look at it through the glasses of the presbyter in 1 Jn and get a very delimited picture. Linguistically the short letters represent a peculiar mixture of Johannine, profane Greek and Jewish-Christian elements. This also applies to the Johannine movement. To the "faithful" in 1 Jn we have to add the fathers of the secessionists – they are best available to us through some parts of the Gospel – and also some who are related to the "brethren" in the Book of Revelation. Elements of futural eschatology in Jn – or in 1 Jn – are not additions in a late stage of the Johannine history but rather remnants from earlier days. Different components of the Johannine movement disintegrated about 100 A.D. in Asia Minor. A limited part of it, the tradition of the presbyter, become the bridge to the Great Church and made the Johannine writings a part of the Christian canon.

---

[19] B. Olsson, *Structure and Meaning in the Fourth Gospel.* A Text-linguistic Analysis of John 2:1–11 and 4:1–42 (Lund, 1974) 255f and 275–279.

The Gospel of John as Gospel Writing

Aage Pilgaard

1. *Definition of a gospel writing*

If one raises the question of the Gospel of John as a gospel writing, no adequate answer can be given unless one takes a stand on how to interpret the term "gospel writing". In other words, we face the question of "gospel writing" as literary genre. Furthermore, this question is not only a literary question, because the answer may also have an influence on a historical and theological evaluation of the genre "gospel writing".[1] An increasing number of articles and monographs characteristically touch on the question of genre after several years of consent as to its definition, the result being that the question must be said to have been set moving in our times. If a clear definition is to be achieved, however, it is important that one specifies the criteria upon which one wants to decide the question of genre, and how one wishes to understand the concept of "genre" in general. It may be understood as a descriptive principle of classification or as a generative pattern of organization, the latter representing the form critical understanding of the kerygma as the basis of the gospel form.[2]

In recent years D.O.Via[3] has combined this interpretation with a structural definition of the gospel genre as tragicomic. To the form critics the following were the major criteria for determining the gospel genre: content, form, origin and purpose (function). The gospels were collections of originally orally conveyed tradition material of various types created to support the message proclaimed through the kerygma. In this way, the gospel writings come to form a new genre. The importance of this genre appears from the fact that John, in spite of his variation from the Synoptists, pursues the same basic pattern.

As for redaction critical research, this focuses on the efforts of the gospel writers, not so much in the literary field as in the theological.

---

[1] D. E. Aune, "The Problem of the Genre of the Gospels: A Critique of C. H. Talbert's What is a Gospel?", *Gospel Persectives*. Studies of History and Tradition in the Four Gospels II (ed. R. T. France and D. Wenham; Sheffield, 1981). W. S. Vorster, "Kerygma/History and the Gospel Genre", *NTS* 29 (1983) 87–95, claim that the problem is historiographical and not literary (p. 92). However, the question of literary genre is also a question of the relation between text and reality.

[2] M. Dibelius, *Die Formgeschichte des Evangeliums* (5th ed., Tübingen, 1966) 8–34; C. H. Dodd, *The Apostolic Preaching and its Developments* (London, 1944) 7–35; cf. *New Testament Studies* (Manchester, 1953) 1–11; J. Schniewind, *Euangelion* (Gütersloh, 1927).

[3] D. O Via, *Kerygma and Comedy in the New Testament* (Philadelphia, 1975).

Furthermore, this involved increased attention paid to a gospel's unity, as presented by a gospel writer. A clear example of this is provided by W. Marxsen[4], an example that also illustrates the terminological muddle, when he determines to let only the Gospel of Mark be an actual gospel writing. In such a case one cannot speak of a genre.

An interesting attempt to throw some light on the history of development of the gospel genre is made by the two researchers H. Köster and J.M. Robinson.[5] They continue with classic form criticism in so far as they see a close connection between kerygma and gospel writing. However, they insist that differing kerygmatic accounts and Christological confessions have existed, and that they have left their trail both within various prestages of the present gospels and within the canonical gospels and finally within the apocryphal gospels. In our context, it is especially important that they isolate an aretalogical literary form which is supposed to have preached Jesus as "theios aner", and which is to be found in part behind a number of miracle stories in the Gospel of Mark, and in part behind the "semeia" of the Gospel of John. On the other hand the literary form leading to the canonical gospels has the form of a Passion Narrative. A gospel writing takes shape, then, when the two forms (genres) are combined by Mark. At a later stage, John undertakes a similar combination under different circumstances.[6]

With their investigations of the history of the gospel genre Köster and Robinson have once again launched the question of the analogy to the gospel genre. More recently, several attempts have been made to find analogies to the canonical gospels from both the Jewish as well as the Greco-Roman world.[7] When including such analogies the question once again becomes relevant as to the interpretation of the concept "genre". If we see it as a principle of classification we will undoubtedly find a number of similarities between the biographical literature and the canonical gospels. However, should we interpret genre as a generative principle of organization, such analogies become more doubtful. A. Dihle expresses the difference as follows: "Hier (in the Gospels)

[4] W. Marxsen, *Der Evangelist Markus* (Göttingen, 1956) 77–101.

[5] J. M. Robinson, *Entwicklungslinien durch die Welt des frühen Christentums* (Tübingen, 1971). Note in particular pp. 20–66, 147–190, 223–250.

[6] Cf. *ibid.*, 223–250, and J. M. Robinson, "On the Gattung of Mark (and John)", *Jesus and Man's Hope I* (ed. D. Y. Hadidian a.o.; Pittsburgh, 1970) 99–129.

[7] Cf. H. Cancik, "Die Gattung Evangelium. Das Evangelium des Markus im Rahmen der antiken Historiographie", *Markus-Philologie* (ed. H. Cancik; Tübingen, 1984) 85–113; C. H. Talbert, *What is a Gospel? The Genre of the Canonical Gospel* (Philadelphia, 1977). Cf. the survey by R. Guelich, "The Gospel Genre", *Das Evangelium und die Evangelien* (ed. P. Stuhlmacher; Tübingen, 1983) 185–204.

erscheint ein Menschenleben als unvergleichbares, unwiederholbares Stück Geschichte, in der spezifisch griechischen Biographie hingegen als individuelle Verwirklichung von Möglichkeiten, die eine unveränderliche Natur für alle Zeiten bereithält."[8]

In his book on ancient Christian miracle stories, G. Theissen presents a remarkable continuation of the form critical opinion of the origin of the gospel genre.[9] He aims at showing how motives of the oral tradition's various forms are present as organization principles in the gospel genre. He refers to an aretalogical, a biographical and a mythical arch. These are arches, i.e. organizing motives, taken from the form of the miracle story, the legend and the myth respectively. By indicating how certain motives function as narrative organization principles he is able to show both similarities and differences among the various instances of the gospel genre. Although each of the four gospels has a combination of aretalogical, biographical and mythical motives, there is a predominance of the aretalogical in Mark, of the biographical in Matthew and Luke, and of the mythical in John.

Ole Davidsen has, however, criticized G. Theissen for overlooking the fact that the mythical structure is the dominant feature also in the Gospel of Mark.[10] According to Ole Davidsen, Theissen's mistake occurs because Theissen overlooks the fact that there are several levels in the narrative progression of the gospel. There is the mythical level dealing with the God-Jesus relation, and there is, according to Ole Davidsen, a "ritic" level, i.e. the Jesus-disciples relation. The extent of the mythical level stretches from the baptism of Jesus to his death and resurrection. The mythical level can end only here because the voluntary death of Jesus happens in obedience to the contract agreed upon at his baptism. God must therefore fulfil his part of the contract and raise Jesus to eternal life.

The relation between kerygma and gospel narrative is explained by Ole Davidsen in the sense that he refers to a "narrative kerygma", which is an organizatory structure, organizing any known kerygma, incompassing the formulas which are concentrated, the narrative kerygmas, and the gospel writings which are expanded, narrative kerygmas. Ole Davidsen hereby overcomes the problem as to deciding which was first: the kerygma or the narrative. From a semantic perspective, there is in

---

[8] A. Diehle, "Die Evanglien und die biographische Tradition der Antike", *ZTK* 80 (1983) 49, in extended edition in *Das Evangelium* (see note 7) 383–411.

[9] G. Theissen, *Urchristliche Wundererzählungen* (Gütersloh, 1974) 211–227.

[10] O. Davidsen, "Narrativitet og eksistens. Et religionssemiotisk bidrag til bestemmelsen af den narrative Jesus i Markusevangeliet", *DTT* 49 (1986) 241–260.

fact no kerygma without a narrative and no narrative without a kerygma; they are mutually dependent.

With this background in mind, if I myself should try to define the gospel genre, I would emphasize criteria such as form, content and function. The gospel genre is narrative, its main character is Jesus of Nazareth, it describes his life in a sequential progression framed by the work of the Baptist and the death and resurrection of Jesus, it has a content which characterizes him as the Son of God and the eschatological Saviour and thereby as the fulfilment of the promises given in the Scripture, and its function is to arouse/strengthen faith in this message.

In my view, I have here pointed out at least three major features of the gospel genre: It tells about Jesus of Nazareth (historical feature), it tells about Jesus of Nazareth as the Son of God (mythical feature) and it tells about his appearance as fulfilment of the Scripture (salvation-historical, eschatological feature). All these three features are present in the four canonical gospels, even in the gospel of John. Consequently, the Gospel of John belongs to the same genre that accounts for the other three gospels. I hereby wish to claim that the interest in Jesus of Nazareth as a historical person is particulary dominant in the Gospel of John,[11] and that it is an important element in the Christology of the gospel.

2. John's interest in Jesus of Nazareth as a historical person

In his article on the interpretation of the Gospel of John,[12] W. Klaiber draws our attention to the obvious, which is by no means obvious, namely that John forms his writing as a gospel writing, accounting for the life of Jesus from his meeting with John the Baptist up until his death and resurrection (exaltation). This, however, emphasizes how important Jesus of Nazareth is as a historical person to John, something that is furthermore supported by a number of individual observations.

1. To Nathanael Jesus is expressly presented as "Jesus of Nazareth, the son of Joseph (1:45) and Nathanael asks: "Can any good come from

---

[11] The question of historical traditions behind the Gospel of John was formerly dealt with in detail by C. H. Dodd, *Historical Tradition in the Fourth Gospel* (Cambridge, 1963). The later development has been dealt with by D. A. Carson, "Historical Tradition in the Fourth Gospel: After Dodd, What?" *Gospel Perspectives II* (cf. note 1) 83–145. Critical of this is J. D. G. Dunn in *Das Evangelium* (cf. note 7) 314, note 11. However, cf. also W. Klaiber, "Die Aufgabe einer theologischen Interpretation des 4. Evangeliums", *ZTK* 82 (1985) 300–324, who advocates the point of view as one of the backgrounds of the methodical approach to John that one can hardly speak of a narrative or speech composition in the Gospel of John without it having been formed around a pre-Johannine tradition kernel.
[12] Klaiber, *op. cit.*

Nazareth?" (1:46). The scandal regarding Jesus, as supposed to be the bread which had fallen from heaven, is caused by his being "Jesus, the son of Joseph, whose father and mother we all know" (6:42). Such a claim was hard to swallow, even for the disciples (6:60). When Jesus hesitates in going to Jerusalem for the Feast of the Tabernacles his brothers correct him (7:1ff) and when he gets there the complaint against his messianic status is based on his being from Galilee (7:40f).

John is the only gospel writer who uses the rather long inscription on the cross, "Jesus of *Nazareth*, King of the Jews" (19:9b). The first miracle by Jesus takes place during a wedding feast to which he is invited together with his mother (2:1–11). She is also present by his cross, and the final act by Jesus is to appoint her a new son (19:25–27).

2. John emphasizes that the appearance of Logos is the appearance of a man (1:14a), and that he at his death is physically human (water and blood) (19:34). In the same way, he stresses the continuity between the crucified and the resurrected (the exalted). Thomas touches the marks and acknowledges him (20:27).

3. John stresses the presence of witnesses at important events, for one thing, his bodily death (19:35), for another, his encounter with the disciples as the resurrected (21:24). To this corresponds the utterance in the prologue: "And we saw his glory. . ." (1:14a).

As important as it is to John to emphasize that his book is the story of the historical person Jesus of Nazareth, it is equally important for him to stress that exactly he is the Son of God, the Logos.

3. *Jesus of Nazareth as the Son of God, the Logos*

We now embark upon the mythical perspective of the Gospel of John. John has clearly marked this perspective by initiating his book with the message of the prologue about the Logos and his incarnation (1:1–18), which so to speak functions as a hermeneutical key to the reading of the gospel.[13] The thought is pursued throughout the entire gospel, especially through the application of the descent-ascent scheme.[14] The incarnated Logos is the only one who has seen God and who can therefore interpret him (1:18), he is the only one who has descended and who has therefore ascended to heaven (3:13). Yet this unique character is none other than

---

[13] Cf. Klaiber, who (*op. cit.,* 308) quotes Käsemann's functional determination of the prologue as "Ortsangabe für das Evangelium und seine rechten Leser, . . "

[14] Cf. G. C. Nicholson, *Death as Departure*, The Johannine Descent-Ascent Schema (Chico, 1983).

Jesus of Nazareth. This appears in a marked way in the witness to Christ by the Baptist.

John is the only gospel writer who has the Baptist witness after the baptism of Jesus. Consequently, that which happens solely between Jesus and God according to Mark and Luke is included here as the climax of the Baptist's witness. The appearance of the Spirit over Jesus is, so to speak, turned into a sign for the sake of the witness by the Baptist, and it is confirmed by God's voice to the Baptist (1:32–34). Christologically, the main concern of John is therefore to prove that Jesus of Nazareth is God's Son, Logos; to prove both; that Jesus of Nazareth is the person, and that what he is is the Logos. The main topic of the narrative of John about Jesus is to show his being (cf. 20:30f). This is a point of divergence between the Synoptists and John: In the Gospel of John it is first and foremost the being of Jesus which qualifies his words and actions, in the Synoptists it is first and foremost the words and actions of Jesus, which qualify his being.

In my view, this accentuation characterizes the entire substance of the Gospel of John. I shall confine myself to two areas of material: the miracle narratives and allegories and the figurative language as a whole.

4. *Miracles and figurative language in the Gospel of John*

In the Synoptics, the miracles of Jesus are manifestations of power (δυνάμεις), i.e. the actions of the Kingdom of God. In the same way, the synoptic Jesus speaks in parables, which is language that presupposes a movement from picture to matter.

The miracles of the Johannine Jesus are on the contrary signs (σημεῖα), not δυνάμεις. This does not indicate that the Johannine miracles are merely to point away from themselves and to a different reality, but it means that they are focal spots, carriers of a content on a different level.

The same applies for the allegories and the figurative language as a whole. The metaphor and the allegory do not point away from themselves, but in themselves they carry a different content, a content at a different and deeper level. However, it applies to both the miracles and the figurative language that both aspects of the case are important: acts and words in one sphere become carriers of a content belonging to a different sphere. In this way both the signs and the figurative language become the means of mediation between two essentially separate spheres: from above – from below, of this world – not of this world.

It manifests itself in such a way that the nature of the acts and speeches of Jesus is in accordance with the notion of incarnation, because according to John the notion of incarnation neither means that Logos has emptied himself, as Bultmann held by way of analogy with the hymn of the Epistle to the Philippians,[15] nor that sarx has become a transparent receptacle for the Logos, which is Käsemann's view.[16] On the contrary, it means that sarx has become the bearer of the Logos, has become the location of the Logos. A mediation takes place both on the spatial as well as on the personal level.[17]

5. *Spatial and personal mediation*

What happens in the Gospel of John is that there is a mediation between two opposing spheres. The two spheres are "from above" and "from below", "not of this world" and "of this world", "truth" and "lie", respectively. The former sphere is euphoric, the latter dysphoric, the former pneumatic, the latter sarcic, the former sphere is God's, the latter is mankind's.

Jesus' mediation between these spheres is realized not merely by his movement from the one to the other, but this movement also coincides with a mediation in his own person between the two spheres' kinds of being. The interspatial mediation has to happen partly by movement from the one sphere to the other, partly by a personal mediation between the two sphere's kinds of being.

In the Gospel of John this opposition is not understood cosmologically but personally. Mankind loved darkness more than light (3:19). Likewise, the mediation is also understood personally: God's love is its motivation (cf. 3:16).

The interspatial opposition is, however, not totally resolved with the mediation as actualized by the appearance of Logos to the world in the being of sarx, because the interspatial opposition is also personal, i.e. man in the world belongs to the being of sarx. The condition, however, for man to transcend this area is for man to be moved from the sphere of sarx to the sphere of pneuma. Jesus explains this to Nicodemus (cf. 3:3). This transition takes place at baptism (3:5). Even as sarx Jesus is the

---

[15] R. Bultmann, *Das Evangelium des Johannes* (10th ed,: Göttingen, 1968) 40.

[16] E. Käsemann, "Aufbau und Anliegen des johanneischen Prologs", *Exegetische Versuche und Besinnungen II* (Göttingen, 1970) 168 ff.

[17] It is consequently a question of anything but "naive docetism" in the Christology of the Gospel of John (so Käsemann, *Jesu Letzter Wille nach Johannes 17*; Tübingen, 1966, 52); cf. H. Weder, "Die Menschenwerdung Gottes. Überlegungen zur Auslegungsproblematik des Johannesevangeliums am Beispiel von Joh 6", *ZTK* 82 (1985) 325–360, who remarks: Käsemann's theory therefore contradicts "gerade dem Grundzug johanneischer Theologie, welche Himmel und Erde zusammenhalten will" (p. 354).

bearer of the spirit (cf. 1:32–34) as an expression of his Logos-reality. Therefore his words are spirit and life (6:63, cf. 6:68), therefore his acts are revelation of his δόξα (2:11). At the same time a full understanding presupposes the pneuma-reality in the receivers as well.

This is part of the background for the large place taken by the farewell speeches in the composition of John. Here it is evident that the reception of pneuma by the disciples assumes the departure/exaltation of Jesus. This reception of pneuma will enable them to understand that which they do not understand now (14:25f.; 16:12–15, 25–28; cf. 13:7, 14:20).

Such a background is also relevant to the commenting level of the gospel writing where the gospel writer consciously reflects on the distance of the actual events in relation to the time after the resurrection of Jesus (2:22, 12:16 [cf. the Paraclete word 14:26]; 20:9).

The appearance of the Paraclete means that the disciples' sarcic being becomes a bearer of the reality of pneuma, mediating between the two spheres. The question of sphere thereby loses its decisive importance because now the disciples can be in this world, without being of this world, since they are bearers of the pneumatic reality (cf. 15:18f; 17:11, 13–18). The spatial distance is consequently mediated on the personal level of being, namely, not-of-the-world. Yet with this relativization of the importance of the spheres the importance of time is also relativized, which explains to some extent the special shaping of eschatology in the Gospel of John. Just as the category of being is superior to that of action, so is the spatial category superior to that of time; the dimension of time serves the spatial and not vice versa.[18]

6. *The relation between Christology and pneumatology*

One may then ask the relevant question as to whether the earthly mission of Jesus was not quite superfluous. Why was it not sufficient for God to let the Spirit mediate between the two worlds? Why was Jesus to come

---

[18] Cf. the remark at the introduction to the farewell speeches (13:1), he loved them "to the end" (εἰς τέλος), and the concluding word at the cross (19:30) "it has come through" (τετέλεσται), which refers not only to the temporal but to a greater extent to the spatial and personal. He loved them to the utmost point of incarnation, and, "the mediation has been carried all the way through".

One might also mention all the spatial deixis's in the Gospel. Cf. R. Kieffer, L'espace et le temps dans L'évangile de Jean", *NTS* 31 (1985) 393–409, who proves the importance of these things in the Gospel and mentions how John in the relation between Jesus and the Baptist defines Jesus as the one who has come before the Baptist (1:15, 30). However, this has to do with the fact that Jesus comes from above. Cf. 3:31, which interprets the temporal aspect spatially (3:28).

first, when he after all had to leave the world anyway for the Spirit to come? In other words, it is the question of the function and relevance of the incarnation and the passion in relation to pneumatology.

In this field we have to move slightly backwards, viz., to the notion of creation at the beginning of the prologue: "Everything has been created thereby" (1:2). This is a strong claim which seems to be opposing the dualism otherwise present in the Gospel of John. I have implied earlier that the Johannine dualism is not cosmologically but personally determined. It is men who loved darkness more than light because their deeds were evil.

Yet the notion of creation presupposes under any conditions that the world created, in as far as it has been created, is not evil in principle, and correspondingly that man, in as far as he is created like sarx, is not evil in principle. The appearance of Jesus as sarx is an affirmation of the somatic, even a restitution of it. As Jesus returns/is exalted by giving this sarx up to death he fulfils the abandonment of the barrier between pneuma and sarx, because he himself gives up his pneumatic-sarcic existence, thereby making it a possible reality for mankind (cf. 19:30).

I am positively inclined to considering the possibility of discovering some kind of notion of atonement in the Gospel of John (cf. 1:29, 36; 10:11). However, I must here confine myself to stressing the importance of the bodily character of Jesus in this connection as well.

The appearance of Jesus is important in yet another way: the appearance of Jesus, indeed even more than that, his sarcic appearance and his death are not only the presuppositions for the advent of the Spirit but also the criteria and material for the activity of the Spirit. The Spirit has no other material than that which Jesus has said (16:14).

Thus, the incarnational as criterion shows through in the ecclesiology of the gospel. I shall confine myself to referring to the sacramental: Rebirth happens not only through spirit but also through water and spirit (3:5); eternal life is obtained through eating the flesh and blood of Jesus (6:53, 58). In this regard one may also note the rebuilding of the temple by Jesus which is the temple of his body (2:21). No matter how one chooses to interpret this we must admit that it means that persons of flesh and blood can worship in spirit and truth (cf. 4:21–24).

7. The story of Jesus of Nazareth as fulfilment of Scripture

The Gospel of John is also a gospel writing in the sense that it has a clear relation to another text, viz., the Old Testament. Just as important as it is for John to define Logos as the historical Jesus of Nazareth, it is equally important for him to classify him as the Messiah promised in the Scriptures (Moses and the Prophets have written about him, 1:45; 5:39, 46).

Furthermore, John shares the conviction with the other gospels that the Scripture is only understood correctly when it is seen in the light of the history of Jesus (2:22; 12:16; 20:9), he is familiar with the Scripture in both its promising and legalistic functions, and he clearly makes the first superior to the latter (cf. 1:17).

The emphasis on Jesus as originating from the Jews, because salvation comes from the Jews, matches the role of the Old Testament in the gospel (cf. 4:8, 22).

The activities of Jesus are characteristically concentrated in Jerusalem and he is summoned there over and over again by Jewish feasts. Especially remarkable is the fact that Jesus' initial and final stay in Jerusalem both occur in connection with the Easter Feast, and that as early as at the initial Easter Feast Jesus speaks of his death which then follows at the final Easter Feast.

In the light of this, one might pose the question as to whether these feast times together with their location do not form part of the Christological sign-interpretation of the gospel, as René Kieffer has indicated.[19]

8. *The function of the gospel*

I initiated this survey of the Gospel of John by emphasizing that the historical person, Jesus of Nazareth, plays a major part in the gospel. In this respect it is important that the author of the gospel is conscious that he has made use of the written medium. It is furthermore characteristic that the author in this connection mentions the signs accomplished by Jesus (20:30f). Why only the signs? Advocates of the source theories – and they are many, both advocates and theories – will answer: They have been taken over from a sign source/sign gospel. This, however, does not solve the present problem.

I mentioned earlier that it is primarily the being of Jesus which qualifies his acts in John, whereas, the acts witness to the being of Jesus in the Synoptists. How can this be consistent with John ending up by emphasizing the signs that Jesus did?

The answers must be as follows: Firstly, the fact that John refers to the signs expresses an insistence on the reality of incarnation: that Jesus of Nazareth is God's son, Logos. Secondly, it is the Logos being of Jesus which qualifies the signs; consequently they can lead to belief. Thirdly, the first act of Jesus as the incarnated one was a sign through which he revealed his δόξα. This adds up with the fact that the last sign by Jesus is the appearance of the glorified in the body of him who was crucified and spear-pierced. The identity of the crucified and the exalted one, of Logos and sarx is thereby pointed out.[20]

This is exactly the point which the author (authors) intends to witness to. His (their) evidence characteristically meets us both in connection with the incarnation and in connection with the resurrection. In connection with the incarnation it was said, "And we saw his glory, a glory like the only begotten from (his) father, full of mercy and truth" (1:14b), and in connection with the meeting with the resurrected one we then get the intention of this gospel. The author (authors) intends to call for/ strengthen belief in this reality from the conviction that the logos-qualified life is in this reality.[21]

9. *The background of the gospel*

One may ask the following questions: Why does Jesus of Nazareth as a factual historical person play such an important part in the Gospel of John? And why is it of such importance to show that he revealed his glory during his earthly lifetime?

In general, I am quite sceptical of attempts to jump to comprehensive conclusions regarding the situation of a gospel writing on the basis of form and content. There are, however, clear indications of violent debates between Jesus and the Jews even in the gospel itself, and these debates are always rooted in the being of Jesus. What gives offence is that this Jesus, whose origin is known, should be God's Son, "the bread of life" (cf. 6:41f).[22] Furthermore, it is characteristic that the prologue ends up by opposing Moses and the Law, on the one hand, and Jesus Christ and mercy and truth, on the other, and then concludes by stressing that Jesus Christ is the only one who has seen and can interpret God. J.D.G. Dunn[23] indicates that the situation of the Gospel of John may have been

---

[20] Cf. the somatic aspect in connection with Mary Magdalene's encounter with the Resurrected (20:17).

[21] According to J. D. G. Dunn, "Let John be John" *Das Evangelium* (cf. note 7), 309–339, Christology in the Gospel of John is Christology "from above". Perhaps so, but it is a Christology which has come down to earth.

[22] In this connection it is quite interesting to note that stichometrically the main caesuras in the Gospel of John according to F. G. Lang, "Kompositionsanalyse des Markusevangeliums", *ZThK* 74 (1977) 1–24, lie at 7:1 and 13:1 (when 7:3–8:11 and 21 are excluded). The debate on Christology reaches a culmination in chap. 6 and then Jesus leaves Galilee for good.

[23] Cf. note 21.

such that conceptions of Jewish theology of an apocalyptic, mystical and wisdomary nature have influenced Christian thinking, including the Johannine. In connection with the Pharisaic-Jewish restoration in the latter part of the century, however, these conceptions are met with heavy criticism, a criticism which also affects Christians to a large extent. It is blasphemous to mention a person like Jesus of Nazareth as the heir of the high positions which are meant, for instance, for Wisdom or the Law.

In such a situation it must have been of decisive importance to stress, on the one hand, the incarnation, Logos became human, and this happened through Jesus of Nazareth, and on the other hand, the creational glory of Logos as having really materialized itself in this figure: "And we saw his glory, a glory like the only begotten from (his) father, full of mercy and truth" (1:14b). Christology, however, poses an inner-churchly problem in Johannine circles: this appears when the gospel is compared with the First Epistle of John. This may be specifically seen in the insistence on the incarnation (cf. 4:2; 2:22f). In this situation the shape of the Gospel of John is once again striking, since it emphasizes both sides of the incarnation: Logos and sarx.

In the first section of my lecture I touched on the question of the relation kerygma and gospel writing. At that point I mentioned the opinion of Ole Davidsen that both kerygma and gospel writing are realizations of a virtual kerygmatic structure in a respectively concentrated and expanded (narrativized) edition. With regard to the relation between kerygma and gospel narrative, the Gospel of John is especially interesting because we find the Johannine theology introduced both in the gospel genre and in the epistolary genre. A comparison between the two genres confirms that there is a close tradition-historical connection between kerygma and gospel narrative as well. In my opinion, the comparison also shows that behind all the variations in the kerygmatic accounts there lies a narration about Jesus of Nazareth, and that this unity is explicitly or implicitly behind all the kerygmatic formulations. Köster and Robinson seem to neglect this side of the matter, and they therefore have no problem in splitting the gospel genre up the way they do. In the gospel genre, however, this is present like a biographical, generative structure. The characteristic feature of the shape of the gospel genre as presented in the Gospel of John is the encapsulating of this frame-account within a mythical narrative frame. This encapsulation creates a paradigmatic field of meaning which influences the entire form, content and course of the gospel.

Roles of Women in the Gospel of John

Turid Karlsen Seim

Next to the Gospel of Luke, the Gospel of John offers rich material, both in quality and quantity, for examining the roles of women in Early Christianity.[1] The present article, however, will not primarily deal with the historical implications but concentrate on describing the internal role pattern in the text of John's Gospel as we know it. There is more to women's perspectives than just focusing on particular women in a fragmentary way, isolating the individual women found in the text and making "a list" of them.[2] It is also important that apologetic or utilitarian interests should not be allowed to become dominant. The main issue is not to prove or refute that "Jesus (or Luke or John or whoever) was a feminist".[3]

The article is therefore an attempt to outline some significant female features in the picture as a whole and as far as possible in an article of limited extent to indicate a coherent view of the roles and functions of women in the Gospel of John. My emphasis is on description rather than on explanation, the description not being dependent on any specific terminology or methodological frame of reference. Some may regard this as a fundamental weakness and an obstacle to real insight; but I prefer to keep the freedom and mobility of an eclectic approach, maintaining as far as possible the gospel text as a meaningful unity.

---

[1] The references and repeated comparisons with the Gospel of Luke in this article are due to various reasons. It has long been acknowledged that among the synoptic gospels Luke is closest to John, and they both have far more material concerning women than Mark and Matthew. However, the main reason lies in my own work on the male/female complementarity and exchange within the role-pattern of Lukan ecclesiology. Most of what is said about Lukan passages refer to this work. So far, only a small part of it has been published (in Norwegian), "Mellom lys og skygge. Kvinners andel i Åndens gave hos Lukas", *Spiritualitet* (F. S. Anna Marie Aagaard; Århus, 1985) 41–53.

[2] L. Swidler, *Biblical Affirmations of Women* (Philadelphia, 1979) has gathered a lot of material, but is a very typical example of this compiling approach. J. Blank, "Frauen in der Jesusüberlieferungen", *Die Frau im Urchristentum* (ed. G. Dautzenberg, H. Merkelin, K. Müller; Freiburg, 1983) 9–91, and K. H. Schelkle, *Der Geist und die Braut.* Frauen in der Bibel (Düsseldorf, 1977), both come close to the same approach. It applies even more to more "edifying" and popular literature as that of J. Nunnally-Cox, *Foremothers.* Women of the Bible (New York, 1981); D. Pape, *God & Women.* A fresh look at what the New Testament says about women (London, 1976) and E./F. Stagg, *Women in the World of Jesus* (Philadelphia, 1978). The excellent integrated and inclusive approach of E. Schüssler Fiorenza, *In Memory of Her.* A Feminist Theological Reconstruction of Christian Origins (New York, 1983), makes the difference in methodology very clear.

[3] Alluding to Leonard Swidler's famous article, "Jesus was a Feminist", *Catholic World* 214 (1974) 177–183.

Historical background and tradition criticism are occasionally drawn upon when needed to determine the actual emphasis of a passage. But within the limitations of this article I am hesitant to infer from text to socio-historical background. This means that I do not presuppose that the roles of women as described in the text correspond to or mirror without reservation a practical function in a specific historical situation.[4] I admit, of course, that historical conclusions may be challenging and that in the last resort they may be desirable and even necessary. But to get there is a long path to tread – with great methodological care – and in any case the first part of it goes through the text as such. The search for a certain "Sitz im Leben" has to take into consideration the total approach of the text and not merely account for various fragments (or isolated females).

With these preliminaries in mind, we may turn to read the text, asking for the roles of women. Does the Gospel of John feature any specific reasons for such a quest as this? Does the question strike the gospel text in important and central passages or does it just graze some marginal points? Are we searching for the bashful little bird in the shadow of an elephant (to use a comparison once made by Krister Stendahl), and have to find our answers by reading contrary to the intention of the writer or to the urging of the text itself? Or may it be that asking for the roles of women genuinely coincides with an explicit interest of the Gospel of John itself, very visible on its textual surface?

In my view, the latter is the case. There is no need to light a lamp and sweep the house and seek diligently in every nook and corner to find the women in the Gospel of John. They are not to be found in passing remarks only, and they are not, as in Mark, concentrated in those parts of the story where male disciples are no longer present. The relevant material is extremely rich and consists of large, literary and theologically complicated passages to be reckoned among the highlights of the gospel. Even more than in Luke, women are main actors in scenes that are quantitatively dominating and of great theological importance. Furthermore, they are presented as having a remarkable singleness of purpose, acting with a kind of striking intentionality and decisiveness.

The passages (and women) in question are as follows: 2:1–12 (the mother of Jesus); 4:4–42 (the Samaritan woman); 11:1–44 (Martha and Mary); 12:1–8 (Mary and Martha); 19:25–27 (the mother of Jesus, her

[4] R. E. Brown, "Roles of Woman in the Fourth Gospel", *TS* 36 (1975) 688–699, and S. M. Schneiders, "Women in the Fourth Gospel and the Role of Women in the Contemporary Church", *BTB* 12 (1982) 35–45, tend to relate some individual features of the text too easily to an estimated socio-historical situation of congregational life.

sister Mary the wife of Clopas, and Mary of Magdala); 20:1–18 (Mary of Magdala). The story now placed in the text of John, Jn 7:53–8:11, is omitted due to its very uncertain position according to the witnesses.

There is no doubt that in these passages one or more of the person(s) mentioned is/are female. It is evident both from how they are characterized and, most frequently, also from their names. Yet we have to consider rather carefully whether the aspect of a person's sex is in any way emphasized and really matters to the understanding of the text. Does it play any role at all whether these persons are women and not men? Or is John's rendering of the gospel-story so inclusive that man or woman makes no difference?

Female inclusiveness, independence and individualization

In her interpretation of the Gospel of John, Elisabeth Schüssler Fiorenza tends to exclusively emphasize the inclusiveness of John.[5] Regardless of sex women and men function inclusively as examples of discipleship both for men and women. With good cause she underlines the inclusive terminology employed by John: the plural ἀδελφοί, μαθηταί used instead of οἱ δώδεκα (cf. in the resurrection-story) and the preference for τέκνα over υἱοί (cf. 1:12 and 11:52).

As already mentioned above, it is indeed remarkable how as a matter of course women throughout the gospel appear as central and well-known actors in the story. They are not presented as dependent on or subordinate to men's authority, but as acting on their own.[6] Like everyone else in the gospel they stand back for Jesus only, as he is the ultimate authority for all. The women are almost always favourably designed, even if they also in the Johannine way seem to "misunderstand" the words of Jesus.

At the same time, there is an impressiv individual differentiation and originality so that each of the women is presented as a person in her own right with a distinctive stamp and, apart from the mother of Jesus and the Samaritan woman, with a name. The general impression given by the synoptic tradition of a group of women (female disciples) following Jesus is apparently toned down in John in favour of an individual specification. It is, however, clear that this Johannine individualization also implies a representative function if not a symbolical one.

There is, none the less, the remaining question as to whether the women are mainly undisputable and representative examples of disciple-

---

[5] Fiorenza, op. cit., 323ff.
[6] To this and the following see Schneiders, op. cit., 38f.

ship as such, or whether the specific point that they are women is explicitly reflected in the text. In what follows I will give my main reasons for assuming that the "sexual" aspect is of importance, and that to fully understand the roles of women in the Gospel of John one has to take this aspect into account.

"Woman, what have you to do with me?"

Two things especially make my position very clear, and they also give evidence of how remarkable and controversial the positions and roles assigned to women in the gospel actually were.

1. In the scene with the Samaritan woman (Jn 4:4–42), v.27 reveals that the (male) disciples marvel, "are shocked", when they come back and discover Jesus conversing with a *woman*. It is noteworthy that they, as might be expected, are not shocked because the woman is a *Samaritan*, although that is what takes the woman herself by surprise when Jesus first approaches her at the well, cf.v.9. In v.27 the theme of antagonism between Samaritans and Jews seems totally to have vanished. The focus is solely on the female sex of the Samaritan as the essential point of difference and scandal.

Rather ingeniously, however, it is also made clear that the disciples know better than to explicitly state their criticism. They keep their reaction to themselves, and we learn only what they were thinking. Their criticism is not voiced because it implies a criticism of Jesus. But as readers we are in this way presented both with objections that might be raised and with the argument for not offering any objection. It appears as a kind of muted communication, revealing and covering up at the same time.

From this strange double communication we learn a) how very unusual and almost shocking it has been to behave towards women as Jesus does in the scene at the well of Jacob, implying a new role pattern for men and women; b) that some even within the community of disciples have reacted against this, but c) that it has been secured by the undisputable authority of Jesus himself. The unconventional role taken up by the woman is an adequate response to Jesus' approach. This follows from the fact that in John 4 he addresses her first – the initiative lies with him.

2. In most of the passages listed above one will find the address γύναι, 2:4; 4:21; 19:26; 20:13, 15. In John men are very rarely addressed at all and never correspondingly. Twice men are called by name (11:43 and 14:9). This happens to a woman for the first time in 20:11–18. At the

empty tomb Mary Magdalene is addressed as γύναι, first by the angels in the tomb (v.13) and then in very similar terms by Jesus himself in the garden (v.15). Still not recognizing him, she responds, believing him to be the gardener. When Jesus then no longer addresses her γύναι but calls her by name (v.16), this transition brings about her recognition of him. Alluding to 10:3–5, she is in this way presented as one of Jesus' own, knowing his voice as he calls her by name. So the transition from γύναι to Μαριάμ signifies an ultimate integration closely connected with Jesus' death and ressurection. This is, however, a matter to be explored later.

Γύναι is first used in 2:4 in the much-discussed word of Jesus to his mother at the wedding in Cana.[7] Does the use of γύναι add to its total effect of distance and dismissal or not? Many maintain that γύναι does not enhance the negative effect of the utterance as it is not supposed to be a particularly impolite address. They quote the other passages mentioned above as evidence that this was the way Jesus usually addressed women, and find it supported also by the synoptic tradition (Mt 15:28; Lk 13:12 and eventually Jn 8:10). Beyond that, there is some evidence in ordinary Greek usage. But all the same, it seems to have been rarely used in the more intimate family sphere.

It is therefore a fact that the γύναι pure and simple is a rather cool way of addressing one's mother. And in this connection it is no argument to the opposite effect that the dying Jesus in 19:26 again addresses his mother γύναι in a situation otherwise determined by care and consideration. Very often the interpretation of this instance is loaded with the interpreters' own sentimental presuppositions of what a dying son may say to his mother.

The use of γύναι in 19:26 reflects rather that the distance indicated in 2:4 is still maintained. The Son's unity is with his Father, and it is the will of the Father (and not the mother) that governs and decides the will, the acts and the life of the Son. I therefore agree with Heikki Räisänen in his concluding remarks on 2:4: "Das Wort gynai betont, dass Maria keine Sonderstellung einnimmt, sie wird den anderen Frauen des Evangeliums an die Seite gestellt."[8] I would, however, like to add that the common use of γύναι also shows a common emphasis on femaleness in these passages.

The mother of Jesus and the family of believers

It is significant that John never gives the name of Jesus' mother – contrary to Räisänen's slip of the pen in the passage quoted above. In the

---

[7] See H. Räisänen, *Die Mutter Jesus im Neuen Testament* (Helsinki, 1969) 161ff.
[8] *Ibid.*, 162.

two passages where she occurs in the gospel, she is just called "the mother of Jesus", and thus her identity is always established by her relationship to Jesus. This creates a certain tension between the intimacy implied (mother) and the distance marked off (γύναι), and indicates that the story develops the true understanding of her motherhood through this tension.

In this connection some attention must be paid to an interpretation presenting Mary (the mother of Jesus) as the new Eve.[9] This network of interpretations appears as a jungle growth of exegetical conjectures and catchword combinations. And it raises a fundamental methodological question: how much or how little is needed of a clue in the text to mobilize comprehensive and complex mythological ideas as the horizon of thought revealing the hidden meaning of the text?

The interpretation (s) claims that the lack of the name of Jesus' mother in John indicates that she (and also the beloved disciple) is primarily a symbolic figure, especially in 19:25–27. In the term γύναι/γυνή one sees an allusion to Gen 3:15, and then ascribes to John the implicit notion that on Golgatha the head of the snake is bruised by the seed of the woman. Mary, the mother of Jesus, is the new Eve (cf. γυνή in Gen 2:23) and "the mother of all living" (Gen 3:20). The figure of the woman clothed with the sun in Rev 12 provides part of the evidence. In John this should imply that the mother of Jesus through the act of Jesus on the cross becomes the mother of all believers represented by the disciple whom he loved.

In this highly speculative interpretation the role of the mother of Jesus becomes not a representative role of women but a position that is unique to her, universal and related to salvation.[10] It is significant that the mythological Mariological interpretation was turned down by the majority of the ecumenical commission of New Testament scholars working on "Mary in the New Testament".[11]

Räisänen has convincingly proved that this theory is based on a heavy over-interpretation of the passage in 19:25–27, and that it ignores the use

[9] For a presentation see Räisänen, *op. cit.*, 176ff; and *Mary in the New Testament. A Collaborative Assessment by Protestant and Roman Catholic Scholars* (ed. by R. E. Brown, K. P. Donfried, J. A. Fitzmyer, J. Reumann; Philadelphia, 1978) 189f.

[10] This applies also to other mariological interpretations, see Schneiders, *op. cit.*, 37: ". . . whatever role Mary is assigned in the Fourth Gospel, it is either unique to her or universal, in neither of which cases is it more significant for women than for men. John does seem to imply that the Mother of Jesus had some special role in relation to the salvific work of Jesus. . ."

[11] Even though the decision was not unanimous, and they leave the door wide open by a rather cryptical reflection on methodology: ". . . the fact that some scholars do accept this symbolism, including at least one of our members, betrays the difficulty of setting limits to symbolism in a Gospel that tends toward symbolism and signs." (190).

of γυνή elsewhere in the gospel.[12] I am, however, less convinced when Räisänen rejects that the scenes in the gospel where the mother of Jesus appears have any symbolic ecclesiological implications at all.[13] In my view they represent a special Johannine version of how the *familia Dei* through a new pneumatic birth/rebirth takes the place of a family relationship defined by the flesh (σάρξ). Jesus' answer to his mother in 2:4, "Woman, what have you to do with me? My hour has not yet come", indicates a distance and a certain dismissal; Jesus' mother does not as mother have any particular claim on Jesus. The absurdity of his rhetorical question – what she has to do with him is of course that she is his mother! – turns it into a sharp refusal in need of an explanation. In the last part of the utterance Jesus actually explains his denial by a reference to the governing will of his life – the way he has to go towards 'the hour' to fulfil the will and the aim of the Father. The mother must give way to the father (cf. 6:42) and his mother accepts this submitting her will to his: "Do whatever he tells you!" (2:5).

Aage Pilgaard has shown by analysing the transformations taking place within the various codes in 2:1–11 that the transformation of the alimentary code and the ritual code (water to wine) corresponds to a change of the genetic code.[14] The presence of Jesus' mother at the very opening of the story implies that he is qualified as a human person of flesh and blood. When Jesus through the transformation of water to wine manifests the doxa by which he is qualified as the Son of God, another transformation is involved, namely the transformation from son of "Mary" to Son of God. The dialogue between Jesus and his mother is the surface expression in the story of this transformation of the genetic code. Jesus' answer establishes a distance between him and his mother and maintains the intimate relationship between him and the Father. But not only does his mother accept the distance and his superior authority, she urges the servants to accept it, too. She enters a new role and becomes a mediator.

This exposition is specific to John. But the subject matter is nevertheless closely related to the synoptic rendering of Jesus' relation to his physical family, particularly the Lukan version. In Lk 8:19–21 Jesus, surrounded by his disciples, rejects the demands made on him by his genetic family, his mother and brothers (i.e. the same family members as

---

[12] Räisänen, *op. cit.*, 176f.
[13] *Ibid.*, 178f.
[14] In an unpublished working paper on John 2:1–11 presented in one of the groups at this Nordic symposium on John.

in Jn 2:12).[15] In this specific scene the synoptic tradition does not name his mother either – as it does elsewhere. The focus is not on her person but on her motherhood. Jesus challenges the claims of his genetic family by converting the categories of kinship to a new group: "My mothers and my brothers are those who hear the word of God and do it." His family are those living in the same obedience as himself. Compared to Mark and Matthew, Luke renders the statement of Jesus in an abbreviated version more inclusively of his genetic family. His mother and brothers are replaced by the *familia Dei*, but are supposed to find their place in the new family. Thus the main point is not to exclude the person of his mother, who has the role of an ideal disciple in Luke, but rather to transform and transfer kinship categories to the community of disciples. Even the maternal rights which were essential to a woman's identity and status are revoked and replaced by discipleship as the new form of motherhood.

In the Gospel of John the Cana-story does not take us that far. As pointed out previously, the replacement is not yet offered. The distance is indicated and so is the priority of "the hour" and the will of the Father. Jesus' mother seems to accept this and enters a role of mediation. But the genetic kinship is apparently not yet broken up; in 2:12 Jesus' mother and his brother are said to come with him – together with the disciples but apart from them. In 7:3ff, however, when members of the physical family reoccurs, the unity still maintained in 2:12 is falling apart. His brothers are said not to believe in him and by tempting him they act as his opponents. This marks a split not only between them and Jesus, but also between them and their mother, who reappears together with her sister in the crucifixion scene in 19:25–27.

The women at the cross seem to be a fixed part of the tradition – although it varies as to which women are mentioned (by name). Martin Hengel has convincingly argued that Mary of Magdala among the female disciples has the same priority as Peter among the male.[16] She is mentioned in all the lists of names, and in the synoptic tradition she heads the lists. In Jn 19:25 the mother of Jesus and her sister are mentioned before Mary of Magdala. Even though the fact that she is included at all is significant and shows her prominent position, preference in Jn 19:25 is given to kinship.

[15] I assume that ἀδελφοί here means "brothers" and not inclusively "sisters and brothers", as "the mother" represents the female disciples.
[16] M. Hengel, "Maria Magdalena und die Frauen als Zeugen", *Abraham unser Vater* (F. S. Otto Michel; Leiden, 1963) 243–256.

In the synoptic tradition the presence of the women at the cross introduces their continuous role in the crucifixion, burial and resurrection story. They witness to the death of Jesus, to the place he was buried and to the tomb found empty on the morning of the third day. They are the connecting link and represent the continuity confirming that it is the crucified and buried Jesus whose tomb is empty. They assure the continuity between the crucified Jesus and the risen Lord.

In John this aspect of witnessing is weakened and almost lacking. The women and the disciple whom Jesus loved are mentioned before Jesus dies and not after, and there is no point in discussing whether they remained to witness his death or not. At the burial only Joseph of Arimathea and Nicodemus seem to be present. In John no one but the risen Lord himself bears witness to the continuity: the resurrected Jesus appears with the crucified body. Apart from in his first appearance to Mary in the garden, the risen Lord makes a point of showing the disciples the marks of crucifixion on his body. In the appearance to Thomas this is emphasized to the extreme before it is modified and corrected by the word about believing without seeing.

Before concentrating on the resurrection stories, something more has to be said about the scene at the cross in 19:25–27. In his structuring of the crucifixion sequence Raymond E. Brown has shown that this is the central scene, the pivot around which the surrounding material turns.[17] It holds a key position in the whole crucifixion drama. Therefore it cannot be reduced to an aetiological note explaining that the mother of Jesus stayed after his death with the beloved disciple.[18] Neither is it adequately explained as a legitimation of the beloved disciple and an enhancement of his authority by relating him to the mother of Jesus – making him Jesus' adopted brother.[19] This interpretation may, of course, catch one aspect of the function of the passage, and if so, it is an interesting point to note that the primary authority lies with his mother, i.e. the woman. Interpretations where the mother and the beloved disciple primarily are seen as figures symbolizing more abstract concepts (as Gentile and Jewish Christianity) or as mythological characters are in better agreement with the key position of the scene in the crucifixion sequence.[20] But, as mentioned above, these interpretations are for other reasons met with conclusive objections.

[17] R. E. Brown, *The Gospel according to John* (London 1966, 1976) 911.
[18] See *Mary in The New Testament* (note 9) 210.
[19] Räisänen, *op. cit.*, 179f.
[20] The various proposals are presented in *Mary in The New Testament*, 214ff, and Räisänen *op. cit.*, 175ff.

When related, however, to the passage in the gospel where the mother of Jesus previously appeared (2:1–12), the significant scene at the cross seems to resume and accomplish the kinship theme: the replacement we missed in the transformation of the genetic code in 2:1–12 is implemented by the exalted Jesus on the cross. The aspect of compensation is evident in the crucifixion scene. 7:3ff made clear that there is a split in the family of Jesus, as his physical brothers do not believe in him. When the beloved disciple is given to the mother of Jesus as a son, she receives a compensation not only for the Son leaving her for the Father, but also for the sons who do not believe. She is included in a kinship community of believers. This applies correspondingly to the beloved disciple. In both cases they are entrusted to each other's care. Through the exaltation of Jesus the inclusive family of God is procreated and born of the Spirit. It also signifies that when he is lifted up from the earth, i.e. on the cross, he is drawing all to him (Jn 12:32). It is thus noteworthy that they are standing close to the cross and not at a distance as in the synoptic tradition.

The mother of Jesus, accompanied by the two other women, and the beloved disciple represent the female and male disciples of the family of God, (re)born through the death/exaltation of Jesus so as to become the children of God. Both the use of kinship terminology and the way in which the two in 19:26f are handed over to each other implies that a strong social structure is established. The new family represents a social alternative, a "counterworld" replacing the one they have had to leave behind, something necessary for their survival in this world. This fits in with a reading of the Gospel of John emphasizing that the social background of the gospel is a situation of crisis where the believers are excluded and excommunicated from their previous religious and social context (cf. the term ἀποσυνάγωγος in 9:22, 12:42; 16:2) and where families are split (9:22f). In replacement they are offered new relationships, a new family with family members tied together in mutual responsibility and kept strong through this interdependence and internal solidarity, their mutual love.[21]

The monumental scene in 19:25–27 thus communicates that Jesus on his way to the Father, in the moment of his "hour", creates/gives birth to the new family of God consisting of "mothers and brothers". The image of birth is used in the Gospel of John in two different ways and places –

---

[21] J. Nissen, *Budskab og konsekvens*. Etiske grundholdninger og konkret praksis hos Jesus og de første kristne (Århus, 1985) 183f with references to K. Wengst, *Bedrängte Gemeinde und verherrlichter Christus*. Der historische Ort des Johannesevangeliums als Schlüssel zu seiner Interpretation (Neukrichen, 1981).

but in both places it is closely related to the death of Jesus. In Joh 3 the figure of rebirth from (water and) spirit pervades the dialogue with Nicodemus; in 16:21 the image of a woman giving birth illustrates the experience of the disciples when Jesus leaves them to go to his Father. Their grief and sadness will be turned to joy when he sees them again, and no one shall rob them of their joy.

In a strange way these two usages of the image of birth converge in the resurrection stories in Jn 20:11–23 where a transformation from grief (tears – water?) to joy is followed by the gift of the Spirit. The tearful grief of Mary of Magdala is repeatedly underlined – before her recognition of Jesus seems to stop her from crying. But it is nevertheless significant that "joy" is not explicitly mentioned until v.20, where the disciples (an inclusive term!) are said to be filled with joy when seeing the Lord. Immediately afterwards they are given the Holy Spirit. Are we witnessing in these two connected stories a birth from water and spirit made possible by the exaltation of Jesus?

In Jesus' word to Mary in 20:17 there is a combination of covenant ("my God and your God") and kinship ("to my brethren", possibly "brothers and sisters", "my father and your father") terminology with a predominance of the latter. It may be that kinship terminology more easily than covenant terminology could be used inclusively. The kinship terminology in this verse also reflects an increase of intimacy between Jesus and the disciples – from servants to friends (15:15) to sisters and brothers (20:17). The transition from γύναι to Μαριάη, discussed above, exemplifies the same progression. However, Mary's responding address, ῥαββουνί does not correspond adequately. She sounds as if she has not yet adjusted to the new terms of relationship, and this may explain Jesus' rather rude admonition to her: μή μου ἅπτου. . ." ("Don't cling to me, I have not yet ascended to the Father"). This rather deprecating remark[22] has some resemblance to Jesus' response to his mother in 2:4:

τί ἐμοὶ καὶ σοί, γύναι; οὔπω ἥκει ἡ ὥρα μου.
μή μου ἅπτου, οὔπω γὰρ ἀναβέβηκα πρὸς τὸν πατέρα.

The new family unity is dependent on Jesus' ascension to the Father revealed as both his father and theirs. Thus, the family of God, consisting of mothers and brothers, knows one Father only. It is constituted not by the mother of Jesus as the mother of all believers but through the ascension of the Son establishing the universal Fatherhood of God and giving birth of the Spirit.

---

[22] The meaning (and translation) of it has been widely discussed, see Brown, *Comm.*, 992ff.

The witness of Mary Magdalene

In the synoptic tradition Mary Magdalene (of Magdala) is the main witness to the empty tomb together with some other women. In John the women's part in the story of the empty tomb is diminished. Of the synoptic group of women only Mary of Magdala remains and she has to share her experience with Peter and another male disciple.[23] But in the Johannine story of the empty tomb there is a strange and rather entertaining apportionment among the persons involved. It makes sure that none of them becomes "the winner" of the search. Each of them is given some priority, and only when their various pieces of evidence are gathered together does the witness become complete. Provided that a prominent position in the resurrection story may be connected with an authoritative and prominent position in the Christian community,[24] this apportionment among Mary of Magdala, Peter and the beloved disciple could imply an egalitarian interest in the leadership of the Johannine community. Authority, witness and proclamation were shared responsibilities including both women and men (Peter as well as Mary Magdalene). The tension and contrast that exists in the synoptic tradition of the empty tomb between the group of women disciples and the men is not be found in John.

In John's version Mary of Magdala is the first to have "seen the Lord", and she is the first to be entrusted with the proclamation of the risen Lord. This is why Mary of Magdala in the Early Church could be mentioned as Apostola Apostolorum.[25] The Samaritan woman has also been honoured by some church fathers as an apostle to Samaria. For our interpretation of John these patristic references are, of course, of less importance. But still they show an unexpected acknowledgement of the role of the women in these stories.

The mission of the Samaritan woman

As pointed out previously, the story in John 4 about Jesus and the Samaritan woman implies a new role pattern for men and women based on the initiative and authority of Jesus himself. Indeed, the impression of

---

[23] When Brown, "Roles of Women...", 692f, maintains that John revises a tradition about Peter by giving to a woman a role traditionally associated with Peter, he underestimates the well-established role of Mary Magdalene in the tradition of the empty tomb. It is far more likely that the Johannine version represents a merger and an equalization of one tradition focusing on Peter and another focusing on the women (Mary Magdalene).

[24] See Hengel, *op. cit.*, 251f.

[25] Brown, "Roles of Women", 693 n 14.

borderlines being crossed is even strengthened in v.27 where it is made very clear that the unconventional behaviour is met with more or less muted reactions.

At the outset of the story the Samaritan woman's coming to the well to draw water involves the mere carrying out a daily errand for a woman. The apparent normality of the situation is altered by Jesus' presence at the well and his approaching her. Her daily and womanly function of fetching water forms the point of departure for their gradually more elevated theological conversation. At first Jesus asks her a favour. But very soon this is turned the other way around, because she, a Samaritan woman, is taken aback by such a request from a Jew. So far, the emphasis is, as noted before, mainly on the traditional antagonism between Samaritans and Jews. The fact that she is a Samaritan *woman* is a scandal that remains implicit until v.27.

It is, however, significant that when she is introduced in vv.7–9, the juxtaposition "Samaritan woman" is repeated three times – obviously stressing the importance of the double qualification alienating her from him/them. The gap between them is thereby drastically widened; as a Samaritan woman, she appears as the essence of Samaritan impurity. Raymond E. Brown refers to a Jewish regulation of A.D.65–66 warning that no one could ever count on the ritual purity of Samaritan women since they were menstruants from their cradle.[26] And the dimension of impurity is implied in the wording in v.9c: "For Jews 'use nothing in common' (συγχρῶνται) with Samaritans." Whether she is to be considered as a loose woman as well is less certain. Many exegetes have paid much attention to this question, seemingly assuming that a woman who has had five men, has to be of easy virtue.[27] They do not sufficiently take into account that matters of marriage and divorce were primarily men's privilege, and that the point of Jesus' statement is not to expose her morals but to show his prophetic power through his miraculous knowledge of her special situation.

Apart from the fact that the conversation between Jesus and the Samaritan woman in itself represents an offence against public decency and rules of purity, it develops into a theological discourse supposed to surpass the mental capacity of women. But Jesus' self-revelation to her (i.a. including the first ἐγώ εἰμι utterance in the gospel) leads to an increasing understanding and recognition on her part. Furthermore, it is hardly an accident that a main issue of the conversation is the replacement of the worship on the mountain and in Jerusalem by the worship in

---

[26] Brown, *Comm.*, 170.

[27] Some have also interpreted it allegorically, see Brown, *Comm.*, 171.

spirit and truth. It envisions a new worship where the antagonism between the different groups is eliminated, and where the exclusiveness of the *fathers' worship* (v.20) have given way to the inclusiveness of *true worshippers* (v.21 where the woman explicitly is included).

The conversation is interrupted by the return of the disciples. Although their scepticism as to what is going on remains unspoken as we have seen above, the challenge is explicitly stated in the text: "What do you wish, or why are you talking with her?" In the following verse a response is immediately provided by the woman herself going into resolute action. She is in a rush, and forgetting why she first came to the well, she leaves her water jar behind. Encountering Jesus has changed her role, and the remaining part of the story presents the woman in her new role within a referential framework of calling and mission.

The woman leaving the jar behind resembles a common feature in the calling stories in the synoptic tradition. Immediately responding to the call of Jesus, the disciples leave everything behind to follow him. And when the woman in v.29 says to the people in the city, "Come, see. . .", it sounds like an echo from the disciples' summons in Jn 1:35–51 (especially vv.39 and 46). For the last part of the story Raymond E. Brown has shown something similar with regard to mission terminology.[28] "Traditional" synoptic figures of mission (harvest) and a more specific Johannine mission terminology are intermingled.

The Samaritan villagers believe because of the woman's words: διὰ τὸν λόγον τῆς γυναικός (4:39, cf. Jn 17:20). In 4:42 this seems to be modified when many more believe because of the word of Jesus himself. They are no longer dependent on the woman's word. Yet this is scarcely to be regarded as a repudiation of the woman so that her word in itself was not good enough and Jesus had to step in. Brown sees it more generally as an expression of "the inferiority of any human witness compared to encountering Jesus himself".[29] But there is more to it than that. Mission in the Gospel of John is not reaching out, but collecting and bringing to Jesus, a gathering into one the scattered children of God as expressed in 11:52. Even at the outset of the gospel story in 1:35–54, the few disciples called by Jesus himself immediately start calling others to come and see, and they bring them to Jesus. In the light of this the Samaritan woman is assigned a missionary task and the transition from the woman to Jesus in 4:42 means that she fulfilled it.

---

[28] Brown, "Roles of Women. . .", 691, taken up by Fiorenza, *op. cit.,* 138, 328 and Schneiders, *op. cit.,* 40.
[29] Brown, "Roles of Women. . .", 691.

The inserted conversation between Jesus and the disciples in 4:31–38 emphasizes and interprets the missionary function of the woman and her pioneering work.[30] While she is calling the Samaritans to Jesus, and as they, called by her, are coming out of the city and approaching Jesus at the well (vv.30 and 40), he tells the disciples to lift up their eyes and see how the fields are already white for harvest. She has sown and they may reap; she has laboured and they may enter into her labour. Mission, too, is a shared labour and responsibility including both women and men. In this sense the contents of vv. 31–32 convey an elaborate response to the sceptical reaction of the disciples in v.27. It becomes very clear indeed what Jesus wanted and why he was talking to the woman. Whatever this may have meant in reference to the history of the Samaritan church, it gives some insight into the problems and prerequisites of shared leadership and partnership in mission.

The missionary function of the Samaritan woman is obviously a public role, and in addressing both women and men (cf. i.a. the inclusive τοῖς ἀνθρώποις in v.28) her work is not confined to a female context. This is different from Luke where women in functions like this are confined to the house, i.e. the private sphere, and/or to work among other women. In the Gospel of John the opposite seems to be the case: women are leaving the house(s) and even Mary of Bethany has to go outside when the Teacher is there and is calling for her (11:20, 28ff).

The confession of Martha and the service of Mary

The raising of Lazarus from death is the last sign of Jesus in the Gospel of John and a compositional zenith. Both in the first sign story at the wedding in Cana (2:1–11) and in the last at the tomb in Bethany (11:1–46) women play a significant role. Martha's opening words in 11:21f are analogous to those of the mother of Jesus at Cana (2:3,5). She indicates the problem without explicitly making a request; the sovereign independence of Jesus is maintained.[31] Lazarus is less important than his sisters Martha and Mary. He is identified through his relationship to them and referred to by name after them in relation to Jesus in 11:5.[32]

The two sisters, Martha and Maria – without Lazarus – are also known from the Gospel of Luke (10:38–42). Some have maintained that the sisters in both Luke and John are depicted in much the same way,

---

[30] *Ibid.*, 691f.
[31] See Ch. H. Giblin, "Suggestion, Negative Response, and Positive Action in St. John's Portrayal of Jesus (John 2:1–11; 4:46–54; 7:2–14; 11:1–44)", *NTS* 26 (1980) 197–211.
[32] Brown, "Roles of Women. . .", 694 n 19.

70

connoting a rather fixed pattern of the different qualities attached to each of them.[33] According to this Martha is restless and active, the practical woman taking care of all the necessary arrangements, while Mary is gentle and a little withdrawn, finding her humble place at the Lord's feet. This is, however, mainly a Lukan picture. In John some of its features may be recognized, but the Johannine picture as a whole is far more intricate. At one point the similarity is nevertheless striking: Martha is very articulate while Mary is silent. Only once does Mary very briefly express herself and she then sounds like an echo of Martha (11:32). Even in 11:39 where perhaps Mary might be expected to respond, Martha suddenly reappears, and the dialogue between her and Jesus is resumed.

The relation between a Martha-strand and a Mary-strand in Jn 11:1–46 and 12:1–8 has frequently been discussed.[34] In Jn 11 the Martha episode is markedly more Johannine than the Mary episode, which may imply that Martha represents the Johannine expansion of a tradition that was more in favour of Mary (cf. the Lukan preference for Mary to Martha in Lk 10:38–42). There are still remnants in Jn 11:1–2 and 45 indicating Mary as the main person. But in the typically Johannine verse 5 where it is related that Jesus "loved" the family in Bethany, Martha is the more important character. She seems to have expanded in the narrative as a main carrier of the evangelist's distinctive theology.[35]

The conversation between Jesus and Martha is of major importance to the gospel story. Full of forebodings and anticipation it ends "the book of signs" and prepares for the passion to come. The secret of death and resurrection is revealed. And Martha responds to Jesus' self-disclosure with the most fully developed confession in the Gospel of John (v.27). Raymond E. Brown has pointed out that Martha in Jn 11 plays a role quite similar to Peter's in the synoptic tradition of the confession made at Caesarea Philippi.[36] Peter's confession in especially its Matthean form (Mt 16:16), "You are Christ, the Son of the living God", has its closest parallel in Jn 11:27: "You are the Christ, the Son of God." In John it appears as Martha's response to Jesus who is revealed to her as the resurrection and the life. Brown regards this as a substitution of Peter by Martha in the same way as Mary of Magdala is substituted for Peter in

---

[33] Brown, *Comm.*, 433.

[34] Brown, *Comm.*, 433; S. M. Schneiders, "Death in the Community of Eternal Life. History, Theology, and Spirituality in John 11", *Int.* 41 (1987) 44–56, 44f n 2.

[35] Schneiders, "Death...", 52.

[36] Brown, "Roles of Women...", 693, developed further by S. M. Schneiders in both articles mentioned (see not 4 and 34), and Fiorenza, *op. cit.*, 329.

becoming the first to encounter the risen Lord.[37] Brown concludes: "Thus, if other Christian communities thought of Peter as the one who made a supreme confession of Jesus as the Son of God and the one to whom the risen Jesus first appeared, the Johannine community associated such memories with heroines like Martha and Mary Magdalene."

In Jn 11 it is significant that Martha's confession precedes the miracle. Before the miracle itself takes place, she has through the conversation reached a clarification and understanding that has the effect of making the miracle almost superfluous. Martha believes even before she has seen. The miracle comes as a total surprise to her (v.39); her reaction against Jesus' order to remove the stone shows this very clearly. The actual raising of Lazarus is an addition mainly aimed at the people – and Mary?[38] – standing by (11:42 and 12:9ff). At the same time the raising of Lazarus is a sign revealing the identity and mission of Jesus. The raising of Lazarus functions in the plot of the narrative as the proximate cause of Jesus' arrest (11:47–50), so that his raising of Lazarus to life means death to Jesus himself. The act is needed for the "hour" to come when his "doxa" can be ultimately seen.

The proleptic perspective of Jesus' death in exalted triumph on the cross is also evident in 12:1–8. The setting of the scene in vv.1–2 depicts a meal where a woman (Martha) serves (διηϰόνει) and the men are waited on (v.2). While diakon-terminology is essential to understand the role of women in the Gospel of Luke, it is, apart from this single reference, totally absent in the Gospel of John. For instance, in John Mary of Magdala has no serving purpose when she comes to the tomb on Easter morning. Thus, the servant role is no main gateway for understanding the role(s) of women in the Gospel of John. But this single reference in 12:2 and the figure of Mary in the same passage entails that it cannot be left out either.

It was part of women's obligations to prepare the food, and within the family they waited on the male members. Whether they also were present serving at parties may have varied, as in some circles it would be offensive for women to appear to men outside the family. In any case meals in antiquity were rather strictly and hierarchically regulated and to

[37] See, however, my reservations to this in note 23.
[38] Schneiders, "Death. . .", 53f, sides Mary with the Jews: "The literary function of the (Mary)episode is to bring onto the stage, with some narrative plausibility, Mary's companions in mourning, the Jews, who will report Jesus to the authorities. . . Mary's function in this narrative is to weep. . ."

wait at the table in a household was a task for those at the bottom, i.e. slaves or women.[39]

The setting in Jn 12:1–2 fits in with this pattern. Lazarus is sitting at the table together with the honoured guests and Martha is busy serving – as in Lk 10:38–42. Some have suggested that Martha in 12:2 is indirectly called διάκονος and thus is presumably performing a eucharistic function.[40] The connotation in the text is, however, very weak, and it is probably too far-fetched. The emphasis is on the humbleness of the act. The impression of female serving and humbleness is strengthened by the act of Mary anointing Jesus' feet.

In the Gospel of John there is no conflict between the two sisters, and their different attitudes/roles are not contrasted as in Luke. The figure contrasting with Mary is not Martha, but Judas. In very different ways both of them prepare ways Jesus for his death. Thereby two sets of values are placed against each other. Mary spends a fortune on Jesus while Judas, being too fond of money, blaims her because according to John he wants part of it for himself.

The sisters, however, are not played off against one another. Each is given a small part in the story of the other sister, thus filling out the picture. They have different leading roles but not in a totally exclusive way. In the preceding story in John 11 Mary was present mourning, weeping and like a silent shadow, a weak echo of the articulate, confessing and believing Martha. At the meal in Jn 12:1–8 the opposite is the case. Mary's anointing of Jesus overshadows the serving of Martha, and Mary is elsewhere actually identified by this act of hers (11:2).

Several elements, which seem peculiar within the isolated anointing story, become meaningful when viewed in the light of the footwashing scene in Jn 13: Mary anointing Jesus' *feet* and not his head, and the ointment that she immediately *wipes* off. When Jesus washes and wipes the feet of the disciples, he is acting towards them as Mary did towards him. This also implies that she in advance has fulfilled his request to the disciples in 12:14f. Her humble role in 12:3ff is assumed by Jesus himself and Christologically mediated as the exemplary role of discipleship, exalting the lowly and reversing the traditional role pattern. While the woman Martha represents the Christological confession and faith of the community, the woman Mary is the prototype of the practice of discipleship.

[39] See L. Schottroff, "Maria Magdalena und die Frauen am Grabe Jesu", *EvT* 42 (1987) 3–25, 12.
[40] Fiorenza, *op. cit.*, 330.

Different Levels in Johannine Imagery

René Kieffer

I use the word "imagery" in a vague sense in order not to be restrained by former ways of thinking, i.e. those adopted when studying proper metaphors in a text.[1] The words we use often refer to objects in the external world. With our senses we perceive reality and develop representations and mental images of that world. We accumulate in our minds representations about, e.g., men and women, about parental authority and, concerning the ultimate reality, about God.

In the word "imagery" I want to include descriptions in a text which we might call "stage-pictures". We know that there are roughly two opposite temperaments: those who think and speak with the help of abstract terms and those who express themselves by metaphors and concrete scenes which they perceive in their minds. The author of John's Gospel is, in my view, typical for this second category of temperaments. When, for instance, he speaks about light he does not use an abstract term. On the contrary, he describes a concrete scene where Jesus appears as the light of the world. To him water is not a worn-out metaphor for spiritual matters; instead he is mentally perceiving Jacob's well or, in the case of the crucifixion, water and blood pouring out of Jesus' side.

Since F. de Saussure we usually distinguish between "signifier" and "signified", *significans* and *significatum*. Where images, symbols or metaphors are concerned we might introduce a further distinction between what is directly signified, *significatum*, and what is indirectly signified, *significandum* or *symbolisandum*.[2] Water is a tangible reality but may signify something vague as life or youth, or something concrete as baptism for the Christians. In John's Gospel Jesus is both tangible and mysterious. Concrete images and stage-pictures help the reader to grasp who Jesus is and what Jesus may mean to him. The author himself says that he wrote down part of the many "signs" which Jesus performed in his disciples' presence, in order that the reader may believe that Jesus is Messiah, the Son of God, and that he may have life through faith in him, cf. 20:30f.

---

[1] A new way of considering metaphors has been proposed by P. Ricoeur, *La métaphore vive* (Paris, 1975). See also his articles in *EvT*, Sondernummer "Die Metapher" (München, 1974) 24–45, 45–70.

[2] Cf. L. Haikola, "Om symboler", *Naturen som symbol*, (ed. J. Allwood, T. Frängsmyr, U. Svedin; Lund 1983) 11–22.

Strangely enough, the cultural background of Johannine symbolic language is described in detail in the commentaries, but few reflections on the connections between images, stage-pictures and Johannine ideology are found there. The latter is properly the object of this short study.

In order not to be too vague I shall begin by presenting five typical scenes. That will permit me to go on to analyzing form and thought in Johannine imagery.

1. *Five typical scenes*

a. To be able to "see", 1:35–51

In 1:35–51 we repeatedly meet expressions which describe a way of "seeing". The Baptist saw Jesus walking by, v.35, and the disciples heard the invitation: "Behold (in Greek: ἴδε) the Lamb of God!", v.36. Jesus turned and saw them following him, v.38. To their question "Where do you live, Rabbi?", he answered: "Come and see", v.39. They went with him and saw where he lived v.39. When Simon arrived Jesus looked at him, v.42. Philip said to the sceptical Nathanael: "Come and see", v.46. Jesus in his turn said to Nathanael: "I saw you when you were under the fig-tree", v.48. The last two verses are a kind of climax: "Do you believe just because I told you I saw you under the fig-tree? You will see much greater things than this!. . . you will see heaven open and God's angels going up and coming down on the Son of Man", vv. 50f.

The reader is implicitly exhorted to join the first disciples, to look at Jesus and to see heaven open. The disciples listen to Jesus' message and are ready to follow him. In a similar way the reader can experience how Jesus' message is addressed to him. The Christian reader knows, he also, that he is seen by Jesus. He has heard about the Christian message, and partially seen Jesus' glory. Nathanael is described by Jesus as a "true Israelite", v.47. Even if John does not insist on the etymology of the word, we come to think of the fanciful interpretation that Philo gives of "Israel": "the man who sees God."[3]

Nathanael will see heavenly visions as did Jacob-Israel, cf. Gen 28:12. Also here, the believing reader who is of Jewish origin can hear a special call addressed to him to become a real Israelite according to the model of Jacob-Israel.

At the beginning of the scene we see the Baptist, standing and giving his testimony about the Lamb of God, v.35. At the end of the scene Jesus opens wide perspectives about what Nathanael will see: "God's angels going up and coming down on the Son of Man", v.51. Before that, we

---

[3] Cf. e.g. *De Mutatione Nominum* 81.

have met different kinds of movements: Jesus walks by, the disciples follow him, inform their friends. In the end, the horizontal axis of coming and going gives way to a vertical event: the angels' going up and coming down. In this way Jesus' profound dimensions are subtly described. The prologue and the Baptist's witness allude to Jesus' pre-existence. In our section we meet the Son of Man upon whom God's angels are going up and coming down. In this way Jesus takes part in the divine sphere.

b. From darkness to light, 3:1–12

One night Nicodemus comes to Jesus, v.2. His visit at that time of the day may be a concrete expression of hesitation. He confesses that Jesus is sent by God, but he has not yet grasped the full truth about this fact. He misunderstands Jesus who speaks about being born again or from above, v.3. While Nicodemus gives Jesus' words a worldly interpretation ("to enter one's mother's womb", v.4) Jesus has a broad perspective of God and the Spirit, vv.5ff. The question about the mysterious origin and direction of the wind, v.8, prepares the issue of the heavenly dimensions which Jesus reveals. The contrast between the things of this world and the things of heaven, v.12, introduces the reader to the vertical dimensions of the Son of man: he came down from heaven and must be lifted up, vv.13ff. Jesus' cross is compared to the bronze snake which Moses lifted on a pole in the desert, v.14. The bitter reality of the cross is associated with an action of giving and sending out from God, v.16. As the world into which the Son was sent can be conceived of as darkness, it is contrasted to light, vv.19ff. At the same time, the author wants to underline God's love for the world, v.16. God's judgement is therefore counterbalanced by God's saving action, vv. 18ff.

The different images strengthen each other: to be sent by God, to be born of water and the Spirit, the things of heaven, to be lifted up, to be saved, to come to the light. Opposite to these themes one has: to enter in one's mother's womb, to be born physically, the things of this world, the snakes in the desert, to be judged, to love the darkness. Men are called to accept the revelation for the sake of which Jesus has been sent to this world.

At the beginning of our text there is night and at the end Jesus speaks about the passage from darkness to light. Whoever does what is true comes to the light and has eternal life.

c. Jesus gives life to those he wants to, 5:1–47

The special technique which the author uses in chapter 5 transforms the healing at the Pool Bethzatha into a kind of illustration of the transformation from death to life. The sick man is healed, vv.9 and 15, but Jesus himself is threatened by imminent death, v.18. Nevertheless, this threat is ineffective, because the Father raises the dead, and the Son can give life to those he wants to, v.21. This theme introduces the consideration regarding the dead who come out of their graves, vv.28f. In a polemic situation the negative judgement on those who do not believe is evoked, v.29 and vv.45–47. The opposite theme is that of the Father's love for his Son, v.20, and the joint life-work of the Father and the Son, vv.17, 21, 26.

The concrete scene at the Pool where a large crowd of sick people are lying and where the paralysed man has no one to put him into the water, is contrasted with the mighty deed of the Son. In a similar way there is an opposition between the praise which the Jews look for and the honour which belongs to the Father and the Son, vv. 23,41,44. Jesus is described as the life-giving Son who is not obliged to observe the Sabbath law, because he himself has the power of life.

d. To be healed from blindness, 9:1–41

The images in chapter 9 are very expressive. Blindness from birth is underlined by the themes of darkness and night. In contrast to this, Jesus is the light of the world and the revealer of God's actions. He concretely spits on the ground and makes some mud with the spittle. Perhaps there is a symbolic signification in this action: the one who comes from above has creative power.[4]

The blind man must also go and wash his face in the Pool of Siloam. The author indicates here that water is of special importance to the miracle. We can guess that it symbolizes Christian baptism, which we already met in 3:5. Baptism can liberate from sin and give a new birth, cf.9:2f, 34.

The water of Siloam was used during the Feast of Booths. People were invited to rejoice when they drew water out of the wells of salvation, cf. Is 12:3.[5] According to 7:37, whoever is thirsty should come to Jesus and drink. When the evangelist mentions that Siloam means "Sent", 9:7, he is probably alluding to Jesus who is sent by the Father, cf. 9:4. Thus,

---

[4] Cf. Irenaeus, *Adversus Haereses* V, 15:2 and Job 10:9 "Remember that you made me from clay" (Hebrew: "like clay").

[5] In the *Mishnah*, Sukkah 4:9, the water-libation, during seven days is mentioned: "They used to fill a golden flagon holding three logs with water from Siloam" (= the fountain of Gihon). The water is taken to the Temple through the Water Gate. When the procession passes that gate, one hears the *shofar* three times. According to the *Babylonian Talmud*, Sukkah 48 b, this is done, because the Scripture says: "Therefore with joy you shall draw water", Is 12:3.

Jesus is included even at the Pool of Siloam as the one who can heal mankind of spiritual blindness; and through him mankind can be reborn by faith. Baptism and faith are joined together in the Christian tradition: one is converted and then baptized in the name of Jesus.

The way in which the man born blind gradually discovers who Jesus is, cf. vv.17, 33, 38, is strongly contrasted with the spiritual darkness into which some Pharisees and Jews fall back. While light is completely given to the blind man, the Pharisees are captured in their sins. The reader is implicitly exhorted to avoid their attitude and to join the faith of the blind man.

e. From death to life, 11:1–53

The story about Lazarus is very rich in different kinds of images. The result of Lazarus' illness is, and at the same time, is not death. Jesus describes his friend, both as one who has fallen asleep, v.11, and as one who has died, v.14. The reason for this is that Jesus has his own conception of life and death. The passage from death to life has its correspondence in those who surround Jesus and who are either believers or non-believers. This is particularly clear when, on the one hand, Martha and Mary confess their faith in Jesus (inspite of Lazarus' death, vv.21f; 32), whereas, on the other hand, some critically say: "Could he not have kept Lazarus from dying?", v.37. Lazarus in his tomb embodies the power of death. When after Jesus' loud call he comes out and is free from his grave clothes, he illustrates the freedom which Christian faith can give.

It is not by chance that Jesus alludes to the twelve hours of the day when people do not stumble, and to the night when it is normal to stumble, vv.9f. Among mankind Jesus is performing the work of daylight, cf. 12:35f. Those who walk with him do not stumble, because they see the light of the world. When Lazarus is brought to life, he symbolizes the light which the faithful get from Jesus. They can see and walk without stumbling.

But the death and the raising of Lazarus also foreshadow what will happen with Jesus himself. After a few days of hopeful expectations Lazarus finally dies. In a similar way Jesus will soon go up to Jerusalem and die. The people think that Mary is going to the grave to weep there, v.31. After Jesus' death another Mary, from Magdala, goes to the tomb, crying, 20:1, 11. When Jesus is deeply moved by the death of Lazarus, 11:33, we come to think of what he says in the prospect of his own death: "Now my heart is troubled", 12:27.

There are also contrasts between Lazarus' and Jesus' situations: Lazarus has been buried four days, 11:39, but Jesus' body is raised on the

third day, cf. 2:19f. The revivification of Lazarus is only a pale anticipation of Jesus' own resurrection. And when Mary gets up and hurries out
to meet Jesus, she too foreshadows the meetings with the risen Christ.
She says to Jesus: "Lord, if you had been there, my brother would not
have died!", 11:32.

To her sister Jesus himself had said: "I am the resurrection and the
life", 11:25. In a kind of foot-note in v.2, it is specified that Mary is the
one who poured the perfume on the Lord's feet, and thus prefigured
what would be done on the day of Jesus' burial, cf. 12:7.

The reader is thus invited by a very rich stage-picture to believe in
Jesus who will soon die and rise again. The glory which the Son of God
will receive according to 11:4 is fulfilled when through his death and
resurrection Jesus "brings together into one body all the scattered
people of God", 11:52.

2. Form and thought in Johannine imagery

The five typical scenes which I have briefly presented can, together with
other material, be an adequate starting-point for some reflexions on
Johannine imagery. "Form" and "thought" are here used in a broad
sense. Under "form" I consider the frame-work and the technical
devices of the evangelist (= a-c below). With "thought" I mean the
message or the ideology of the author (=d).

a. The implied reader

In the five scenes we can see how subtly the reader is implied in what is
described.[6] In the first scene he is invited to be in his turn a disciple who
can "see" what Jesus stands for. The scenes with Nicodemus and the
blind man implicitly exhort the reader to open himself for the Spirit and
the light which Jesus brings. In the scenes with the paralyzed man and
with Lazarus the possibility of being healed from sin, sickness, and death
is evoked.

Other Johannine scenes have a symbolic signification for the reader.
The cleansing of the Temple and Jesus' comments on this action are not
understandable until the Resurrection, 2:13–22. A Jew at the time of
Jesus could understand that the Temple made of stones had to give way
for the spiritual temple. But only the Christian believer who has received
the Spirit from the risen Lord can discover a metaphor for Jesus' body in

---

[6] I use the word "implied reader" in a non-technical sense, comprehending both the
"narratee" and the properly "implied reader". The "real reader" can in his turn endorse
the implicit exhortations of the text.

the Temple that has been torn down and built up again.[7] The reader rejoices with the disciples at Jesus' words which they remember and understand.

At the wedding in Cana, 2:1–11, the reader discovers the first manifestation of Jesus' glory together with the disciples. The evangelist makes him aware that this scene foreshadows the time of the cross, when Jesus will fully be given glory.

The Gospel of John is the only canonical gospel which mentions how Jesus' side was pierced by a soldier and how blood and water poured out together, 19:31–37. In the commentaries on this scene, v.35 and even vv.36f are often considered as later additions.[8] However, for the evangelist or at least for the final editor the remarks on the author's testimony and the Scripture's truth are fundamental in order to involve the reader in the scene that has been described.

Thus, we can see how the reader is involved in the stage-pictures, either directly by appeal to his faith, or indirectly by his subtle assimilation into the role of a disciple. Remarks on a later understanding of what happened and an intensive description of Jesus' miracles have a performative function of inducing the reader to accept the evangelist's message.

b. The sign-function of the stage-pictures

The evangelist has reduced the miracles to a minimum of seven or eight, which are partially presented in an over-all perspective. Two enumerated "signs" are performed in Galilee, 2:1–11; 4:46–54. Two miracles connected with each other happen at the Lake of Galilee, chapter 6. It is possible to add to them the risen Lord's function at the miraculous catch of fish in chapter 21. Two miracles of healing are located in Jerusalem, in chapters 5 and 9. The raising of Lazarus in Bethany, chapter 11, which as we have seen points forward to the resurrection of Jesus, can be considered as a climax.

The two miracles in Galilee achieve the result that the disciples and the official and his family respectively believe in Jesus. When Jesus walks on the water people marvel, and when he feeds five thousand men a decisive turning-point has come for the disciples. Those who leave Jesus on that occasion anticipate the greater crisis provoked by the crucifixion. The miracles in Jerusalem lead to several threats of death against Jesus. The

---

[7] Cf. Léon Dufour, "Towards a Symbolic Reading of the Fourth Gospel", *NTS* 27 (1981) 439–456 (esp. 446ff).

[8] See the discussions in R. E. Brown, *The Gospel According to John* (XIII–XXI) (New York, 1970; repr. 1981) 945ff.

raising of Lazarus issues in a definitive resolution to kill Jesus, 11:45–53.

The catch of fish after the Resurrection has a special function of underlining the future work of the disciples. The text is an addition that partially can be based on material of the main author.[9]

There are other stage-pictures which function as "signs" and disclose the faith or the unbelief of the audience, e.g., the cleansing of the Temple in 2:13–25, Mary's anointing in Bethany, and the people's acclamation near Jerusalem, 12:1–19. A special kind of symbolic action is performed by Jesus when he washes his disciples' feet, pointing out the love which leads him to death.

Similarly there are scenes where people meet Jesus and witness for or against him: the Baptist in 1:19–34; 3:22–30; the first disciples in 1:35–51; Nicodemus in 3:1–21; the Samaritan woman and her fellow-contrymen in chapter 4; the Jews at the Festival of Booths and at the Festival of the Temple in chapters 7–8 and 10:22–39; the disciples before and after Jesus' death in chapters 13–17; 20–21. In the overall composition of the Gospel, these meetings often have a symbolic meaning.

After the miracles Jesus is engaged in dialogues as in chapters 6 and 11, or holds a kind of revelation speech as in 5:19–47 and 10:1–17. Twice Jesus takes elements of parables as a starting-point for his self-revelation, 10:1ff and 15:1ff. The imagery in these parabolic speeches has a function similar to that of the miracles in other speeches.

Beside these stage-pictures we have the author's or the editor's remarks on what is happening: longer texts as in the prologue 1:1–18; in 3:31–36, or short notices as in 1:28, 38, 41; 2:11, 21f; 3:24, etc. In his doctoral thesis B. Olsson has studied these different comments.[10] Of special interest for our purpose are those which throw light on the foregoing stage-pictures with the help of a post-Easter understanding, e.g., 2:21f; 12:16; 20:9. We can notice how the ideology in these remarks also is expressed in the different scenes and in the whole Johannine imagery. Beneath the *significatum*-level of the narratives we constantly meet a *significandum* -level, an ideology.

Many things that Jesus does or says have both a pre- and post-resurrection meaning. In order to interpret correctly what is happening or what is said the reader must be helped by the Holy Spirit which Jesus promises for the time after his departure. Events, images, and words are different kinds of signs which lead to a living faith, if one knows how to

[9] Cf. Brown, *op. cit.,* 1077ff.

[10] B. Olsson, *Structure and Meaning in the Fourth Gospel.* A Text-linguistic Analysis of John 2:1–11 and 4:1–42 (Lund, 1974) 259ff.

interpret them correctly. The evangelist himself knows how they must be understood. By describing positive and negative ways of comprehending, he invites the reader to choose the right side and open himself to the Spirit and faith in Jesus.

c. The composition of the stage-pictures
The different stage-pictures are built up with the help of concrete details which obtain a deeper meaning by the discussions or the commentaries which follow. This is clear in our five typical scenes: The disciples see Jesus and are seen by him. The dialogues invite the reader to open his eyes to what faith in Jesus can achieve. Nicodemus is informed about being born again and has to deepen his own understanding of Jesus. The concrete scenes at the Pool Bethzatha, near the Temple in Jerusalem, or in Bethany show us the healing of a sick man, a blind man and a dead. Through the subsequent discussions the reader is then invited to interpret these healing miracles as signs of life, light and resurrection.

Other scenes may be evoked. In Cana water turns into wine. The different dialogues between Jesus, his mother, and the servants, as well as the commentary which the man in charge of the feast addresses to the bridegroom open new ways of understanding what has really happened. The evangelist's remarks help in 2:6, 11 the reader in their turn to consider the miracle as a symbolic action.

In the scene where Jesus cleanses the Temple we are first confronted with his violent actions and after that with disputes with the Jews, which give a deeper meaning to what he has done. The cleansing of the Temple foreshadows the destruction of the Temple, which in its turn symbolizes Jesus' death. The comments of the evangelist in 2:17, 22 invite the reader to see Jesus' resurrection as a sign which allows the master to cleanse the Temple. We can here observe how complicated the Johannine symbolization is: The cleansing of the Temple as a sign of the destroying and rebuilding of the Temple foreshadows Jesus' death and resurrection. Inversely, the dead and risen Jesus illuminates the scene of the cleansing of the Temple.

When Jesus meets the Samaritan woman, part of the imagery is constituted by Jacob's well, and the food which the disciples have bought (=*significatum*). The conversations between Jesus and the woman, and between Jesus and the disciples transform these concrete details into symbols of eternal life and apostolic work (=*significandum*).

In the dialogue between Jesus and the Jews in chapter 6 the miracle of the bread becomes, as a consequence of the miracle of the manna, a sign of the bread of life that comes down from heaven and is identified with the flesh and blood of the Son of Man. A progressive "metaphorisation"[11] is taking place: bread is a metaphor of the one who comes down from heaven and gives life by his flesh and blood.

We meet a similar metaphorical development in the previously examined scene with Lazarus: his death and raising are progressively transformed into imagery that foreshadows Jesus' own death and resurrection. The twelve hours of the day and the night when one stumbles are part of that "metaphorisation". Therefore Jesus can suddenly say: "I am the resurrection and the life". He is also the light of the world which prevents men from stumbling. The images reinforce each other and create a space where the metaphor rules.

d. The prevailing ideology

In a former article I have underlined how, in the Gospel of John, temporal and spatial determinations are often leavened with the question about Jesus' origin and destiny.[12] Space and time are important for locating the stage-pictures. The whole imagery in its turn is taking place in a theological perspective which the evangelist wants to promote: Jesus' overwhelming greatness.

I have repeatedly underlined the vertical dimension in the Gospel's imagery: the angels are going up and coming down on the Son of Man, birth is from above, the Son of Man has come down from heaven and is lifted up as Moses lifted up the bronze snake on a pole in the desert, Jesus has been sent by his Father, etc.

It is easy to find this vertical dimension in the Gospel of John: it demonstrates the uniqueness of Jesus. His greatness is also underlined by comparisons: Jesus is greater than Abraham, 8:53–57, or than Moses, 1:17f; 9:29. He is the bridegroom, whereas the Baptist only is his friend, 3:29. He is the real light, 1:9, the real bread, 6:32, the good shepherd, 10:11,the real vine, 15:1. All these comparisons, which correspond to Jewish expectations, surpass former patterns.[13]

The same thing can be said about the titles which are given to Jesus. He is Messiah and the Son of God in a very special sense. He is the Prophet, the sovereign Teacher, the King of Israel and of the Jews in a deep sense (cf. 19:33ff), the Lamb of God, the Saviour of the world, the Son of Man not only for the end of the world but already as the pre-existent one, the Word which already was with God before the world was

---

[11] On the signification of this "metaphorisation", see the works of Ricoeur mentioned in note 1.

[12] Cf. my article "L'espace et le temps dans l'évangile de Jean" *NTS* 31 (1985) 393–409.

[13] Cf. my article "A Christology of Superiority in the Synoptic Gospels", *Religious Studies Bulletin* 31 (1983) 61–76.

created. In 8:24, 28; 13:19 Jesus can say of himself "I am who I am". Three times he is called "God", 1:1, 18; 20:28. His close relation to his Father is mentioned throughout the Gospel and lends a profound dimension to all imagery.

* * *

It is difficult to analyze the composite nature of Johannine imagery, especially in such a short study.[14] But I hope I have been able to give some insights into the way in which the evangelist works with his material.

Psychologists usually attribute images to man's primary processes. Images come up in our dreams and derive from fundamental patterns in our striving and in our interests.

In John's Gospel the concrete imagery probably corresponds to the author's deep experience. He is not content with underlining Jesus' greatness, which could in the end be tiring for the reader. With the help of stage-pictures and images he gives us a lively expression of his deep faith, that Jesus died and arose as the Saviour of the world. This is for him not a dead tradition which he only transmits, but he himself is reborn by the Spirit of Jesus. That makes him report on Jesus' words and deeds in such a way that the message can become life and truth for the reader.

[14] In my forth-coming Swedish commentary on John I give further examples of Johannine imagery. I hope to publish in French a more systematic study on this subject. The first volume of the commentary has been published in 1987: *Johannesevangeliet 1–10* (Uppsala, 1987).

Johannine Jesus-Belief and Monotheism

Lars Hartman

"He showed me the river of the water of life, bright as crystal, flowing from the throne of God and of the Lamb" (Rev 22:1). Although I will confine myself to the testimony of the Fourth Gospel in dealing with "Johannine Jesus-belief", this passage from the Book of Revelation, nevertheless, illustrates our problem. The phrase "the throne of God and of the Lamb" may raise the question: How monotheistic is the prophet after all? Does he think in a way that reminds of the heretics against whom orthodox Jewish theologians firmly maintained that there are not "two powers in heaven"?[1] Are there two powers in John's heaven? Jesus goes to the Father (14:12, etc.) and prepares a place for his disciples in the Father's house (14:2f); he will do what they ask for in his name (14:13f); he and the Father are one (10:30; cp. 14:10f); an "only God" who is in the bosom of the Father has made God known (1:18); and the Word was with God, and the Word was God (1:1). One asks again: one or two powers?

There are different ways in which this problem may be dealt with. One is not to deal with it at all, i.e. only an account of a number of "ideas" or "concepts" is given from the Johannine corner in the museum of the history of ideas. The problem may also be treated indirectly, in that one connects the different Christological "ideas" or "concepts" with different phases or developments in the history of the Johannine church.[2] Thus it has been suggested that the development began with a Jewish-Christian belief in Jesus as the Messiah, a belief that also implied a debate concerning the Messiahship of Jesus. The next phase, one goes on, involved contacts with Samaritans which led to a Wisdom Christology. This brought the Johannine Christians into conflicts with Jews, the character of which is reflected in statements in the gospel such as this one: "we stone you. . . for blasphemy, because you, being a man, make yourself God" (10:33; cp. 8:58f; 19:7).[3] Thus the difficulty caused by the tension between, e.g., a Messianic Christology and a Logos Christology would have a historical explanation. But this sort of problem is not solved simply by having a theory of its origin. To express it in terms of a

---

[1] SDeut. 379, etc. See further A. F. Segal, *Two Powers in Heaven* (Leiden, 1977).

[2] Cp., e.g., U. B. Müller, *Die Geschichte der Christologie in der johanneischen Gemeinde* (Stuttgart, 1975); L. Martyn, "Glimpses into the History of the Johannine Community", *L'Évangile de Jean. Sources, rédaction, théologie* (ed. M. de Jonge, Gembloux, Leuven, 1977) 149–175; R. E. Brown, *The Community of the Beloved Disciple* (New York, Ramsey, Toronto, 1979) 25–69.

[3] Cp. Brown, *loc. cit.*

possible situation in the early period of the gospel, let us say around 100 C.E. in Asia minor: was the worried monotheistic Jew living next-door content with the soothing explanation of the Johannine Christian, "Take it easy, brother, this difficulty in the gospel has its origin in the attempts of some people in the previous generation to express the significance of Jesus by using Wisdom categories." Very likely his opponent would retort: "But what do you yourself mean when you read this text about Jesus?"

I regard it plausible to assume that the author(s) of the gospel, as well as the reader of it, whom I shall call a "Johannine Christian", were monotheists. They have agreed with Jesus' address of God according to 17:3, "the only true God".

Monotheism was, however, anything but uncomplicated and simple. Take Philo, for example. Of course he is a monotheist. But as self-evidently as other people in his time he assumed that there existed other divine beings than the God of Israel, such as the sun, the moon, and the planets, which, in addition, were not lacking in power. But, Philo argued, they were subordinate gods who fulfilled their tasks by commission from the Supreme God.[4] There were also other subordinate powers in Philo's world, e.g., God's judging power, and the Word, the Logos, creative and maintaining, which like the High Priest stood between God and creation and which also was called God's firstborn.[5]

Furthermore, we may turn to the meditations by some Jews on the heavenly throne as represented in Ezechiel and Daniel or Isaiah, i.e., the Merkabah traditions.[6] They asked themselves regarding who sat on the throne (or thrones) beside the one of the Ancient of Days as pictured in Dan 7. They spoke – or, rather, whispered, for these were awful and deep mysteries[7] – about a being beside the Supreme Being, about Metatron[8] or The lesser Yahweh (3 En 12:5). Against those who stumbled in this regard anathemata were hurled like the one I cited above, "there are not two powers in heaven".[9]

---

[4] Spec. leg. 1.13.

[5] See H. A. Wolfson, *Philo* I–II (Cambridge, Mass. 1948), *via* Index *sub* Power.

[6] G. G. Scholem, *Major Trends in Jewish Mysticism* (1941; New York 1961); Segal, *op. cit.;* I. Gruenwald, *Apocalyptic and Merkabah Mysticism* (Leiden, 1980).

[7] Hag. 2.1; Pesiq. 145b.

[8] See Segal, *op. cit.*, chapter 3.

[9] This is one of the points in J. D. G. Dunn's instructive article, "Let John be John", *Das Evangelium und die Evangelien* (ed. P. Stuhlmacher; Tübingen, 1983) 309–339.

Johannine Christians may very well have been assailed by similar accusations when they referred to the Son of Man as ascending where he was before (6:62) or reported Jesus to have said that he and the Father were one (10:33; 17:22). But regardless of the accusation, how did they themselves think? Did they just heap up these statements without reflecting on them? We should certainly not be too quick to assume that even reflecting Christians necessarily felt a need to analyze traditional language and establish some sort of philosophically justifiable expression of their faith, thus pushing aside the variegated and multifarious traditional expressions. And yet, when living with a text like the Prologue of the Fourth Gospel one is not likely to be theologically and philosophically innocent.

Something that should have contributed to making the issue of monotheism a problematic one is that one did not merely have to explain what had once been remarkable about Jesus. Were it all only about something belonging to the past, the problem would be no worse than in the case of Plato or of Jeremiah or of the Teacher of Righteousness. But Jesus was also somebody to whom the Johannine Christian had a relationship in the present. He was presently alive in some sense in heaven. In the following I shall alternate between these two reader perspectives. On the one hand, I shall ask, how did one possibly think when it came to talking about Jesus who once lived on earth, paying due respect to monotheism at the same time? On the other hand, I shall ask, how could one, remaining true to the same monotheistic conviction, think about the living Lord of whom one now professed oneself an adherent?

I will pose the questions of the preceding paragraph considering some of the more salient Christological designations we encounter in the Gospel of John. This does not mean doing a Christology of "titles". On the other hand, we can discern some different thought patterns or imageries, which function each one by itself, or, more commonly, in combinations, to express what one believed concerning Jesus.

I begin with the Messiah-role and try firstly to regard it as enacted by Jesus within the story of the gospel, the plot of which the Johannine Christian placed in a period about some 70 years back in time, but features of which he may have had to defend against questions or accusations. It is almost trivial to state that believing somebody to be the Messiah did not normally have to imply a conflict with a monotheistic faith. Thus, the Messianic confession of Nathanael should not have been regarded as too bold, "you are the Son of God, you are the King of Israel" (1:49). Such a Messianic belief dit not necessarily assail any monotheism, for within its framework the Son- designation meant that the Messiah functioned on God's behalf, and that his reign or his task had its origin and its legitimation with God.[10]

Regarded in this way the answer in 10:24ff to the question whether Jesus was the Messiah, did not *at first* have to disturb either traditional Messianism or monotheism. The works that Jesus did in his Father's name bore witness to him, it is said (10:25) – no problem is raised so far. Neither did, presumably, the following use of the Shepherd-image cause any difficulties – there is easily room for that imagery within the Messianic pictorial framework. The motif that the Father has given the sheep to him (v.29) is also traditional. Thus, e.g., in Ez 34 God speaks about his sheep, for which he will raise a shepherd, a David who shall feed them (v.23).

But continuing in Jn 10, we encounter a Jesus who crosses the border of the traditional: "I give them (the sheep) eternal life" (v.28), "no one shall snatch them out of my hand" (v.28). The next verses explain why Jesus can do what is normally God's work, viz., giving eternal life:[11] "no one shall snatch them out of my Father's hand. I and the Father are one" (vv.29b–30). To the Johannine Christian who looked back at this debate of older days it might have been possible to defend himself against an opponent who thought that Jesus had been blaspheming (cp. 10:33, 36); he could say that "the Jews of that debate in Jn 10 were wrong in saying 'you, being a man, make yourself God' (v.33)". The defense could go on using the argument of the gospel text, which advances in two steps. First, Scripture itself can call men gods, for in Ps 82:6 it is said, "you are gods". The second step could be paraphrased like this: "actually Jesus, being a man, did not say that 'I *am* God', but the Father had set him apart, had 'consecrated' him and sent him to the world. He was acting by his commission." Such an answer would, thus, argue that Jesus' divinity was attached to that which he said and did rather than to his person.[12] But if the debate of Jn 10 only concerned a function or a divine commission, the Johannine Christian looking back at the past had probably to confess that the Jesus of the gospel did not do very much to calm those who anxiously asked about his monotheistic orthodoxy. The statements concerning his doing the Father's works (10:32, 37) did not lead to the conclusion, "thus I am really acting by God's commission". Instead we read, "believe... that the Father is in me and I in the Father" (v.38), and

---

[10] E.g., F. Hahn, υἱός, *Exeg. Wörterb. z. N. T.* III (1983) 912–937, 916ff. Also J. D. G. Dunn, *Christology in the Making* (London, 1980) 12ff.

[11] R. E. Brown, *The Gospel according to John* I–II (Garden City, New York, 1966–70), I, 407, refers to Wisd. 3:1 and Is 43:13.

[12] See, e.g., C. K. Barrett, *The Gospel according to St John* (2nd ed; London, 1978) 382ff. For a thorough discussion of the background of the idea of the commission concept in Jn see J.-A. Bühner, *Der Gesandte und sein Weg im 4. Evangelium* (Tübingen, 1977).

one must concede that this breaks with a Messianic commission Christology (if I be allowed to use this expression).

Yet the text on the Shepherd-Messiah is written with the present-time of the reader in mind: he is one of the sheep in the Shepherd's flock. In such a present-time perspective the problem of monotheism grows more serious. The gospel reader learns that Jesus once promised eternal life to them who walked in his flock, like Peter and Nathanael. It becomes essential for the reader that this was once true and that Jesus thus really did God's work. For otherwise, the Johannine Christian could hardly believe that two generations later he gave eternal life to him and his fellow-Christians. That is, also in the present-time of the reader there should have been some meaning in the statements "I and the Father are one" and "the Father is in me and I in the Father" (10:38). In the present-time perspective the commission Christology thus went vastly beyond the limits of normal Messianic ideas. But only in this way did the Johannine Christian obtain a Jesus to believe in, one who not only belonged to the past, but one about whom he could also say "my Lord and my God" (20:28).

In Jn we can hardly find any distinct traces of what we could call a continued pursuit of the Messianic categories into heaven. Such a thing can be observed in other Early Christian traditions, especially through a reading of Ps 110 as bearing on a heavenly enthronement.[13] To be sure, we can find a similar mode of thinking in Jn, namely that of the Son's glorification.[14] But this idea is not connected with the role of a Messiah: "I have glorified you on earth when I accomplished the work which you have given me to do; Father, glorify me with you with the glory which I had with you before the world existed" (17:4f). Dare I make the following ultrashort interpretation of the passage?: God is "glorified", i.e. God's "glory", as much of God that men can bear and grasp, was made known through the work of Jesus.[15] This is another way of saying what we came across in the passage on the Shepherd-Messiah, who carried out his commission "in the name of the Father". The commission or the "work" is brought to an end in the Son's death: when he is executed and exalted – lifted up, he is called a king in the *titulus* on the cross (19:19); there is the culmination of his "glorification" of the Father, and the Father "glorifies" him, when he, so to speak, dies to the Father. Here we are at the issue of monotheism again: the Jesus of the Johannine Farewell

---

[13] See, e.g., O. Cullmann, *The Christology of the New Testament* (London, 1959) 222f.

[14] Cp., however, below, on 3:35, and furthermore, note 37 (the Son of Man).

[15] E.g., Barrett, *Comm.*, 166, 318, 450f; H. Hegermann, δόξα, *Exeg. Wörterb. z. N.T.* I (1980) 832–841, esp. 839ff.

speech had a glory in the presence of the Father before the world, and he is said to have returned to that glory, through his death, and to own it again.

How has our Johannine Christian conceived of Jesus' glory with the Father? When, in the Prologue, it is said that "the Word pitched its tent among us" and that "we beheld its glory, glory as of the only Son from the Father" (1:14), it is quite probable that our Christian meant that Jesus' appearance meant a divine presence on earth which could be compared with that of the Shekinah in the Temple. But how did he think of Jesus' glory in heaven, in the divine dimension? According to 12:41 the evangelist seems to suggest that the glory which Isaiah saw (Is 6) was that of Jesus. It is not unlikely that he – and his reader towards the end of the first century – meant that this glory was something like the divine power with which the Supreme Majesty sustained and governed everything, that is, in other words, ideas belonging to the area of Wisdom – or Logos – speculations.[16] But in order to find such a frame of reference for 12:41 we turn in vain to Jn 12; instead we are referred to the Prologue. It means that we also have to admit that the evangelist's use of the Messianic language and his way of speaking of Christ's glorification did not give any substantial help to his reader who asked the same questions as we.

The "Father – Son" combination puts a typical stamp on Johannine Jesus-belief, and this is our next Christological motif to be discussed. We have already touched upon the Son-title in relation to the Messiah. On closer inspection it appears that whereas "the Father" occurs frequently, the gospel speaks of the "Son" almost only in clauses concerning the Son's work in performing the Father's commission.[17] Thus we find ourselves largely within the framework of traditional language: the Father sent the Son to save, in that men believe in him (3:16), he sent him to give life (5:21, 25f), and to judge (5:17).

When the Johannine Christian considered that which was reported as having happened some 70 years ago, he could probably, with some effort, understand most of what was said concerning the Son, without having to be too worried by questions on monotheism. That the Son was sent by God (3:17) did not necessarily have to be understood differently from the statement that John the Baptist was sent by God (1:6).[18] The

[16] R. Schnackenburg, *Das Johannesevangelium* I–IV (Freiburg, Basel, Wien, 1965–84), II, 520; cp. Brown, *Comm.*, 33, 487.

[17] See further Schnackenburg, *Comm.*, II, 150ff.

[18] In fact, however, Jesus is represented as more heavenly than John, in that, so to speak, more than the commission appears to come from God.

commission Christology would also be able to embrace the clause that the Son gives life (5:21); that life is namely given to people who believe what he does and says "in the name of the Father".

In some instances, however, a futuristic eschatological work of the Son is in focus. Here, again, the framework of a commission Christology, as applied to the Jesus of the 30's, is widened, and to such an extent that it bursts. Let me cite two passages, the first of which is 6:39f: "I will raise them up at the last day" (also 6:44, 54). That this "I", the Son, is going to raise the dead at the last day means that he is performing something that is otherwise regarded to be God's work.[19] Thus, the question of monotheism is raised. The author does not give any clear indication as to in which terms he is thinking. If we assume that he creates a realized eschatology out of the traditional statement concerning the raising of the dead at the last day, it hangs together: the revelation of God which the commissioned Son gives means eternal life to the one who believes – he lives even if he dies (11:25f). Then not only the motif of raising the dead has been translated into meaning "the gift of life through faith", but the idea of the last day has also been "demythologized"; it would stand for something like the individual's encountering eternity (in the moment of *Entscheidung* or in his death).[20] But I dare not straightforwardly maintain that this is the thought of the evangelist, and even less so that our Johannine Christian has understood his text in this way. Perhaps he has retained the traditional concepts while at the same time being ready to allow them, partly in tension to each other, to complement one another and together form what we could label a pictorial or symbolic language.

A second Son-passage, which causes some questions as to how the evangelist saves his own and his reader's monotheism, is 14:12f: "he who believes in me will also do the works I do; and he will do greater things than these, because I go to the Father. And whatever you ask in my name, I will do it, in order that the Father may be glorified through the Son." Also in this case the trouble arises because the saying deals with the Son's work after his departure to the Father. This means that the problem is the same, whether our Johannine Christian should try to defend the saying as valid once in the early 30' or he should take it as stating something concerning himself and his heavenly Lord.

It seems that the contents of 14:12f is an expansion of the traditional manner of speaking about the Son as working on earth by the Father's commission. However, this work has now become the Christians' continuation of Jesus' work of revealing the Father, i.e., the mission of the

[19] E.g., Barrett, *Comm.*, 260.
[20] Cp. C. H. Dodd, *The Interpretation of the Fourth Gospel* (Cambridge, 1953) 147ff.

Church.[21] Thus, the Father is also glorified through this continued work. But the way in which the Father – Son combination appears in the text does not provide much help against an accusation of at least a modified bitheism. If our assumption of a basic monotheistic belief on the part of both author and reader is correct, such an accusation would be false. But, as indicated, there are no clear points of departure in the text to explain why there are not two powers in heaven.

A particular group of clauses that relate the Father to the Son (and vice versa) is formed by the statements that the Father loves the Son (3:35; 5:20; 10:17; 15:9; 17:23, 26), and that the Son loves the Father (14:31). In next to every instance this relationship is coupled with the idea advanced against unbelievers, that the Son really performs the work of the Father, indeed, that this love is the basis for the claim concerning the Son's reliability as acting on the Father's behalf. Thus, our Johannine Christian could also bring these passages in under a commission Christology, which did not have to arouse the suspicion of a dubious views on God's being the only true God.

A statement like that of 3:35 might, however, be a little too stiff: "the Father loves the Son *and* has given (perfect tense – δέδωκεν) everything in his hand." Regardless of the traditio-historical or religio-historical origin of the motif,[22] when seen within the framework of the earthly Jesus it renders the commission to Jesus as authoritative as altogether thinkable. Furthermore, when understood in the present time of the Johannine Christian, it is not hard to imagine some raised eyebrows on the side of inquisitive monotheists.

This may be the right occasion to touch upon the statements of the unity of the Father and the Son, which I mentioned briefly when dealing with the Shepherd-chapter.[23] Also in these cases we must state that the point is not ontological but rather concerns the validity of the Son's revelation of the Father and of his work on the Father's behalf. It should also be remembered that the unity of the Father and the Son corresponds to a unity between the Son and the believers. This also holds true for the other manner of expressing this unity, viz., the "in"-phrases, eg., 17:23,

[21] E.g., Barrett, *Comm.*, 460.

[22] See, e.g., R. Bultmann, *Das Evangelium des Johannes* (10th ed;. Göttingen, 1941) 119f; S. Schulz, *Das Evangelium nach Johannes* (2nd ed.; Göttingen, 1978) 67.

[23] See 10:30; 17:11, 22f. Also the reciprocal "in" one another of the Father and the Son – 10:38; 14:10f, 20; 17:21, 23 – see Dodd, *op. cit.* (n. 20) 187ff. Further. T. E. Pollard, "The Father – Son and the God – Believer Relationships according to St John: a Brief Study of John's Use of Prepositions", *L'Évangile de Jean* (see note 2), 363–369. See further M. L. Appold, *The Oneness Motif in the Fourth Gospel* (Tübingen, 1976), discussing the "theology" of the oneness passages on p. 261ff.

"I in them and you in me". C.H. Dodd, in my view, has a fine comment on this passage: "It is not a question of inhering as it were adjectivally in the absolute Substance. God is 'the living Father'. His life is the outpouring of love. Nor is the divine love conceived abstractly. . . It is a radically personal form of life, manifested in the concrete activity of Christ in laying down His life for His friends. . . It is by becoming first the objects of this love, and then in turn the subjects of the same love, directed towards Christ and towards one another, that we become one by mutual indwelling both with the Father and the Son and with one another in them."[24]

Understood in this or a similar way our Johannine Christian would have no difficulties with the unity-passages as long as he thought of Jesus 70 years ago.[25] But, again, in what terms could he think when he also was certain that Jesus was one with the Father now? Once again, we are forced to admit that the passages in question do not indicate any answer to our question.

In four passages the Son is defined as μονογενής (1:14, 18; 3:16, 18; cp. 1 Jn 4:9). The adjective means "only", "unique", and it is hardly fair to the Greek to try to squeeze something out of its second part, viz. the -γενης, as if it should mean "born of the Father" or something similar.[26] However, in one of the four passages there is a "from the Father", viz., in 1:14, in which we read of the glory which is seen in the Logos incarnate, "a glory as that of the only one from his Father". If one understands the Greek in this way,[27] one can put the stress on a revelatory aspect of the verse, i.e., revelation through the incarnate, or on a Christological aspect, i.e., on Christ's heavenly glory on earth.[28] Regarding the former case, one may say that the same thing is said in different words a few lines later in 1:18, "no one has ever seen God; an only (μονογενής) God[29] has made him known".[30] Regarding the latter case one may understand the passage as saying that Jesus "would participate in the divine life and glory by virtue of the eternal love which the Father had for him even

---

[24] Dodd, op. cit., 197.

[25] Dodd (op. cit., 187ff) cites Corpus Hermeticum and Philo for similar ways of talking of men's unity with or indwelling in God.

[26] But cf. Barrett, Comm., citing Dodd (see note 20) 305.

[27] Schnackenburg, Comm. I, 247, attaches μονογενής to παρὰ πατρός. Thus also E. Haenchen, Das Johannesevangelium (Tübingen, 1980) 130.

[28] The alternatives remind of Bultmann's and Käsemann's fight over the passage (E. Käsemann, "Aufgabe und Anliegen des Johanneischen Prologs", Exegetische Versuche und Besinnungen (3rd ed.; Tübingen, 1968) II, 155–180). Cp. Haenchen, Comm., 128f; J. Becker, Das Evangelium des Johannes (Gütersloh, Würzburg, 1979–81), I, 76ff.

[29] Reading θεός instead of υἱός.

[30] Bultmann, Comm., 43f, is not far from such a view.

before the creation of the world (17:24)".[31] For my part, I tend towards accepting the former alternative.

Of course 1:18, just mentioned, also raises questions as to the issue of monotheism and Christology. In v. 17 Moses the Lawgiver and Jesus Christ, through whom grace and truth came, are placed beside each other. Implicitly, then v. 18 represents Christ's superiority as revealer, for, according to Ex 33:18 Moses was not allowed to see God's face, whereas Christ was even in the bosom of the Father. But, when the text says "an *only God*" this conclusion of the Prologue seems to pick up both the Logos-motif from its beginning, i.e. "the Logos *was God*", and v. 14's motif of the glory of the Logos become flesh, i.e. "glory as the *only one* from his Father".[32] Thus, as in so many other instances of the Father-Son constellation, a dominating feature is the unique validity of God's revelation in Christ.[33]

We may also notice that in 1:18, as well as in 1:14, dealt with above, a Son-Christology is combined with a Logos-Christology, although the Son appears here as the μονογενής. With the approach I have chosen it is of some importance that this occurs at the beginning of the gospel, and in such an elevated passage as that. From the reader's point of view (and, why not, for that matter, from that of the "evangelist" or redactor also?) this introductory material colors the message of the text which follows.[34] The Son, then, even less than in the Messianic field of associations, is not God's "boy". Rather he is God's active, creative and salvific intention, expressing itself in Jesus, lived by him. That is, when the richly developed Son-Christology is combined with a Logos-Christology, the Johannine Christian seems to have received a set up of ideas that would help him to maintain the radicalism and the validity of God's revelation in Christ, the man, and also to affirm that this Christ was his Lord and God in the present. And lastly, he could do both and yet claim to be a monotheist.[35]

We now come to a group of verbs which also have to do with the question of John's monotheism. I am thinking of the following ones: to

---

[31] Schnackenburg, *Comm.*, I, 247.

[32] Barrett, *Comm.*, 169.

[33] J. A. Fitzmyer, μονογενής, *Exeg. Wörterb. z. N. T.* II (1981) 1081–1083.

[34] See, e.g., R. H. Lightfoot, *St. John's Gospel* (ed. C. F. Evans; London, Oxford, New York, 1960), II, 78, – I certainly do not deny the legitimacy of traditio-historical investigations, which, in our case, can suggest that because the prologue is assumed to belong to a later stage of the development of the Fourth Gospel, one should not allow it to serve as a clue to other passages, i.e., when one asks for their meaning at an earlier stage of the history of the text. Cp. Becker, *Comm.*, 71ff.

[35] See also Dunn, "Let John be John" (see note 9) 334ff.

be sent, come, descend, come from, be from above.[36] In different ways they say in a mythical language that Jesus had a commission from God to fulfill (an expression which, of course, is also mythical). He had a task, quite as John the Baptist or the prophets or the word which goes forth from God's mouth and does not return until it has accomplished his purpose (Is 55:10f). With these verbs Jesus' work is rooted in God's will. E.g., "I have come down from heaven, not to do my own will, but the will of him who sent me" (6:38). A Johannine Christian would have no difficulties in defending such a statement as put into Jesus' mouth. At least such a one would not question his – or Jesus' – monotheism. But, as we also saw a while ago, when speaking of the Messiah, now and then the pronouncements advance beyond the limits of the undisputable. It is, namely, evident that not only the commission or the message is held to be of divine origin, but also the "I" who carries it. This becomes even more evident in those phrases which stand for a corresponding move-ment to the Father or upwards after the completion of Jesus' work on earth, viz., the verbs 'to ascend, go (to the Father), go away'. E.g., "Now I am going to him who sent me (16:5). . . if I go away, I will send the Paraclete to you" (16:7). The imageries which are the presuppositions of these verbs only partly lend themselves to answering the questions concerning monotheism that may appear, and this is the case in those contexts in which the commission-Christology prevails. However, when the Johannine Christology advances beyond that limit in using these verbs, they do not help us in answering a question as to how the Johannine Christian joined this Christology with monotheism.[37]

We now arrive at the "I am" pronouncements. Of these I shall only deal with the absolute ones, i.e. those which have no predicate. One example is 8:24, "if you do not believe that I am, you will die in your sins", or, a few lines further on, "when you have exalted (lifted up) the Son of Man, you will know that I am and that I do nothing on my own but speak thus as the Father taught me" (8:28).

Several commentators agree in the assessment that somehow the evangelist makes use of a turn of phrase from the Septuagint, particularly from Deutero-Isaiah, where it is used of God himself in a revelation

---

[36] For traditio-historical investigations see P. Borgen, "God's Agent in the Fourth Gospel", *Religions in Antiquity* (*in mem.* E. R. Goodenough, ed. J. Neusner;Leiden, 1968) 137–148, and Bühner, *op. cit.* (note 12).

[37] The Son of Man imagery is, of course, one further element in the Johannine Christology and may be of some importance to its way of relating Christology and Theo-logy, although it is difficult to see any distinct traces of how. Traditio-historical points of view are found in S. Schulz, *Untersuchungen zur Menschensohn-Christologie im Johannesevangelium* (Göttingen, 1957) and Bühner, *op. cit.,* 385–99.

formula.[38] With some minor differences most commentaries also say that the meaning of the phrase is that Jesus is the one who more than any other reveals God. Some intimate that the evangelist makes Jesus designate himself with the Divine Name, indeed, identify himself with the Supreme Majesty.[39] Others deny such an interpretation, pointing to the circumstance that this absolute "I am" is most often followed by statements containing what I have called a commission Christology. Such is the case, e.g., in 8:28, quoted above.[40]

Our Johannine Christian could perhaps maintain an understanding of these "I am" pronouncements in terms of a commission Christology as long as his opponents only wanted to claim that, if Jesus said such things 70 years ago, he had blasphemed. But what happened when he read them as concerning his own Lord and God, now alive? What about the unity of God? It occurs to me that he would agree with the reader of Phil 2:9, "therefore God has exalted him and given him the name which is above every name". But the writer does not give the slightest intimation as to which terms or with what sort of imagery he is thinking, and thus we hear nothing of an enthronement or anything similar. A principal message of the "I am" mode of speech seems to be this one: in the Jesus who lived and worked a couple of generations ago, God was active and communicated himself in a perfectly valid and unique way, and this still holds true, also as something of deeply personal relevance to the Johannine Christian. Some expressions in chapter 17 fit together well with this understanding: "I have revealed your name to men" (v. 6), "keep them in your name which you have given me" (v. 11); "while I was with them I kept them in your name which you have given me" (v. 12). Here "in your name" represents what I called the divine communication of itself. Yet when the speculative and inquisitive mind asks as to how it should think in a Johannine way of, so to speak, the revealer's heavenly status, it is not very much helped by the "I am" pronouncements.

I have already touched on the Logos-Christology, and it seems that it was the means by which our Johannine Christian got farthest in his efforts to keep Christology and monotheism together.[41] On the one hand, it is true that in the Fourth Gospel an explicit Logos-Christology is only found in the Prologue. But on the other, from that position it really determines the total gospel, quite in the same way as the key signature at

---

[38] E.g., Dodd, *op. cit.,* 93; Brown, *Comm.,* I, 533ff; Barrett, *Comm.,* 342; Schulz, *Comm.,* 132. Cp. Bultmann, *Comm.,* 265.

[39] Brown, *Comm.,* 350; J. Marsh, *The Gospel of St John* (London, 1968) 360.

[40] Becker, *Comm.,* 209f; Schnackenburg, *Comm.,* II, 254; Barrett, *Comm.,* 342.

[41] Dunn, "Let John Be John" (see note 9) 330.

the beginning of a piece of music. In addition, it must be remembered that we come across several of the Christological motifs of the gospel precisely in connection with Wisdom: being sent, descending, "I am", light, food and drink, being with God from eternity, indeed, being God.[42] To speak in Antiquity about God's Logos (or Wisdom) meant speaking of God and the world in terms of other dimensions than those used when talking of God in the heavens above over against the world below.[43] God's Logos, or his Wisdom, his intention, his creative, maintaining, life-giving and directing meaning was in, under, beyond and before all things. Many educated and pious people of Antiquity would certainly have been able to follow most of what is said in the Prologue. In fact, a Johannine Christian who defended Jesus' appearance 70 years ago against his Jewish neighbor could hold his ground for quite a while quoting, e.g., the Book of Wisdom: "generation by generation she (i.e., Wisdom) enters into holy souls and renders them friends of God and prophets" (7:27). The view of the Logos as being of eternity with the Supreme Being was good religion. Thus, we may presume that our Johannine Christian also managed to defend himself as being a monotheist against the questions that might be raised by the statement that in the beginning Logos was with God (1:1). But to accept that Logos/Wisdom had become flesh, and not merely had inspired or characterized Jesus the prophet and teacher, that must have been too hard for any dialogue-partner of the Johannine Christian.[44]

Thus, to express it in a somewhat translated form, the Johannine Christian's belief was that God's Logos received its perfectly valid expression in the man Jesus and that it performed itself in him. This is the presupposition behind the claim concerning the validity of God's revelation and self-communication in Christ, and it may well be taken as the framework within which Jesus is called God (1:1, 18; 20:28; cp. 10:33; 5:18). But once again we run into the difficulty for which our previous deliberations have not provided any solution: Jesus prays, according to 17:5, that the Father will glorify him with the glory he had "before the beginning of the world". In the present context it seems best to assume that the expression should be understood by way of adducing the Logos-categories, the Logos who was "in the beginning" (1:1). Perhaps our Johannine Christian would say to a strictly monotheistic philosopher that the wording in 17:5 refers to the eternal Logos on its way to

---

[42] Brown, *Comm.*, CXII – CXXV.

[43] This does not imply that I suggest that the "God above"-language meant that its users thought in naive three-dimensional terms of these matters.

[44] Bultmann, *Comm.*, 40ff; Barrett, *Comm.*, 164f.

accomplishing itself in the last part of its earthly commission as performed by Jesus. But the theologian, both today and in the second century, asks: how are the subjects related? The eternal Logos, accomplishing itself, and the man Jesus who approaches death? Of course these theologians receive no answers from the evangelist.

The same theologians may pose more questions to John. Above I used the expression that 'Jesus died to the Father'. In John's sight the divine Logos realized itself thus. But to this the evangelist joins his faith that Jesus has risen from the dead, a Jesus who from his exalted position sends the Paraclete, etc. Over against this combination the theologian may ask the rash question: how is the risen man Jesus related to the divine Logos? Decent exegetes probably shudder at such a question, saying: one should not ask such questions. Other theologians have also refrained from them, although for other reasons. I think of John Climacus, the 7th century ascetic:

> I asked what the Lord was before He took visible form. The angel could not tell me because he was not permitted to do so. So I asked him: "In what state is He now"? and the answer was that He was in the state appropriate to Him though not to us. "What is the nature of the standing or sitting at the right hand of the Father?" I asked. "Such mysteries cannot be taken in by the human ear," he replied.[45]

In any case we can state that the evangelist seems to have left his Christian reader to rest content with letting the tensions remain: in the man Jesus God's intentions were carried out in a unique way, and there God was manifest as never elsewhere. Furthermore, this was not simply an episode in history but it remained valid and relevant in the present of the reader. The Logos that had been carried out was still a divine reality. But at the same time the Johannine Christian was persuaded that this human person in which the Logos realized itself was now united with the Divine Supreme Majesty, so that 70 years afterwards he could turn in the direction of the divine dimension of the world, above, under, within, beyond the world, and adore him saying, "my Lord and my God". How far he then "demythologized" the language of resurrection we do not know, but probably not in any "philosophical" way. When the Logos Christology was made to color other Christological concepts and combinations of concepts he had a multidimensional picture of his Lord which he was able to hold on to, still being a convinced monotheist. Perhaps we could even say that he thought of Christ in a complementary way, using modes of thinking which stood in tension with each other but

---

[45] John Climacus, *The Ladder of Divine Ascent*, Step 27 (trans. C. Luibheid, N. Russell; Classics of Western Spirituality; London, 1982) 268.

which he thought rendered justice to his belief in Jesus only when used together.

It is not until later that we find theologians trying to bring order into the Johannine tensions and to speak of the two natures of Christ, discussing how one should join such ideas with a monotheistic belief. It was also in later times that it was decided to regard as heretic the more or less subordinationist Christology implied in the teaching of some of the earlier theologians of the Church. In a way, the evangelist gave them something which could serve as a basis for their subordinationism. But he also said things which tended in the opposite direction, e.g., by having Thomas confess, "my Lord and my God".

Thus, we can state that we have put more questions to the evangelist than the text he left behind gives any answers to. As a matter of fact, theologians of our own days also admit that Christian dogmatics still has certain difficulties when it tries to come to grips with the problems we have, in a rather primitive way, dealt with here,[46] problems which were so hotly debated in the struggles of the Ancient Church over Christology and Theo-logy.[47]

[46] See, e.g., J. R. Geiselmann, "Jesus Christus", *Handb. theol. Grundbegr.* I (1962) 738–770, 770, and witness the wrestling in K. Rahner, "Jesus Christus II", *Sacr. mundi* II (1968) 920–957, 948ff.

[47] On the Fourth Gospel and the Christological debates of the Early Church until and including the Arian controversy see T. E. Pollard, *Johannine Christology and the Early Church* (Cambridge, 1970). A massive investigation and collection of material is A. Grillmeier, *Jesus der Christus im Glauben der Kirche I.* Von der Apostolichen Zeit bis zum Konzil von Chalcedon (451) (Freiburg, Basel, Wien, 1979) – see e.g., *via* index *sub* Zwei-Naturen-Lehre.

The Fourth Gospel as Viewed by Fridrichsen, Odeberg and Gyllenberg

Harald Riesenfeld

In the six decades from 1920–1980 three Scandinavian New Testament scholars contributed to the study of Johannine literature in ways which are well worth commemorating. Their works on the Gospel of John form part of much wider interests. But precisely their broad knowledge and extensive work enabled them to discern and to determine specifically Johannine elements of thought and of style.

Anton Fridrichsen (1888–1953) had a reputation far beyond the frontiers of his native country Norway when he was invited to take over the chair of New Testament at Uppsala in 1928.[1] He had studied theology and classical languages at Oslo and in German universities. In 1925 he had presented his doctoral dissertation, "Le problème du miracle dans le christianisme primitif", at the University of Strasbourg. A stream of philological remarks on different New Testament passages flew from his sedulous pen.

During his years at Uppsala Fridrichsen became aware of and paid particular attention to the question of the self-consciousness of Jesus. He became more and more convinced that the confidence of being God's Chosen One, the Son of Man, which Jesus had throughout the time of his public ministry, was a uniting factor not only in different parts of the gospel tradition but also in different streams of traditions and lines of thought in the Primitive Church. There was also an interchange between Messianic ideas in Judaism at the beginning of our era and the ways in which the person of Jesus was looked upon and was understood by his contemporaries. From his understanding of the person of Jesus as pictured in the gospels Fridrichsen was able to add new and capturing dimensions to the sayings and narratives contained in the gospels. The collection of short commentaries on the Sunday pericopes of the Church of Sweden, which were posthumously gathered and edited, is a treasure-mine of brilliant observations on gospel texts.

Hugo Odeberg (1898–1973) pursued his post-graduate studies in London University under the direction of the famous Canon G.H. Box.[2] He acquired a vast knowledge and an impressive command of various Semitic languages. Then he was able to penetrate into Rabbinic and Gnostic texts which had never before been translated or made the object of

[1] H. Riesenfeld, "Anton Fridrichsen", *SEÅ* 18–19 (1955) 7–13.
[2] H. Riesenfeld, "Hugo Odeberg", *SEÅ* 39 (1974) 161–165.

scientific study. The thesis which gave him a British degree was published in 1928 "3 Enoch or the Hebrew Book of Enoch". There Odeberg showed his mastership in two fields, Semitic philology and Jewish mysticism. Having been appointed in 1932 to the New Testament chair at Lund, he continued publishing Hebrew and Aramaic texts and commenting them linguistically. He often returned to the British Museum Library for periods of research work. But gradually he switched over to commenting, in Swedish, New Testament books or selected texts, illuminating not least their setting in a Judaism where normative tendencies did not yet prevail.

Rafael Gyllenberg (1893–1982) came from a Swedish-speaking family in Finland but went to school where Finnish was the predominating language.[3] In 1929 he was appointed to a chair at the University of Helsinki. But when the chair of Biblical exegesis at the Swedish-speaking young academy of Turku (Åbo) became vacant in 1934, he willingly accepted an appointment and served in this position until 1964, teaching Old Testament as well as New Testament. At Turku he was one of the leading figures in academic life, which had to be maintained also during the demanding years of World War II. Gyllenberg was ambitious in keeping up relations with colleagues and friends above all in Germany and Sweden.

Having written two dissertations for a double degree in 1922 (*Pistis*, 1–2), in later years he mainly published commentaries in Finnish and Swedish on various parts of the New Testament. Simultaneously he continued with his Pauline studies and played, in addition to his learned work, an active part in the cultural life of his country.

1. *New light on the Gospel of John*

In the beginning of this century the Fourth Gospel was considered to be of minor interest from a historical point of view. Common opinion held that exclusively the Synoptic Gospels, above all that of Mark, could furnish the material necessary for a reconstruction of the life of Jesus. From such a point of view Johannine literature would be the product of marginal currents in the Early Church, void of substantial traditions from the public ministry of Jesus.

Since then, the outlook on the Gospel of John has changed anew. In many cases information given on topographical or chronological details has turned out to be more reliable than corresponding data in the Synoptic Gospels. Moreover, the outline of the life of Jesus, not least a

---

[3] G. Lindeskog, "Rafael Gyllenberg in piam memoriam", *SEÅ* 48 (1983) 7–9.

duration of two or three years for the public ministry of Jesus, seems to be closer to historical facts than the kerygmatic synopsis presented by the other three gospels.

Among those who have contributed to a new appreciation of the Gospel of John one might mention E.C. Hoskyns, C.H. Dodd, E. Stauffer, J.A.T. Robinson and R.E. Brown. As a consequence, questions about the traditions behind the gospel, influences on its religious thought, the style and purpose of the gospel and not least its proper theology have resulted in new answers.

Therefore the Scandinavian contributions to the study of the Fourth Gospel, which will fill part of the following pages, were made in a period when, from an international perspective, intense research led to new insights and conclusions.

2. A. Fridrichsen

As to the time and place of the composition of the Fourth Gospel, Fridrichsen shared the views which had been prevailing from his younger years.[4] The gospel got its shape about 100 C.E. in Ephesus in Asia Minor, where a Christian congregation had existed for half a century. The author addressed his work to Christian churches in Asia Minor but had the universal Church in mind at the same time. Since Christianity in that period was in a stage of rapid expansion, the gospel must inevitably have had a missionary effect. In I John the author, who was identical with the redactor of the Fourth Gospel, shows himself to have been a powerful and clear-sighted ecclesiastical leader.

The redactor, who deserves the designation Evangelist, got his material from three sources: narratives and speaches coming down from the apostle John; other traditions, mostly oral ones; the Synoptic Gospels. The speeches which are characteristic of the Fourth Gospel, are thematic compositions of sayings (*logia*), on the analogy of speeches in the Synoptic Gospels.

Some of the logia have been handed down in variants (e.g., 14:13, 14; 15:7). With a pedagogical intention some sayings are repeated; 6:39, 40, 44. Sometimes a basic saying has been made the object of an exposition, a commentary (e.g., 16:23–27).

Fridrichsen differed from earlier research when he accepted typically Johannine sayings, especially what he called basic sayings, as genuine sayings of Jesus. The way in which Jesus speaks in the Synoptic Gospels, when he proclaims the kingdom of God, was not the only mode of speech

---

[4] A. Fridrichsen, *Johannesevangeliet* (Stockholm, 1939).

which Jesus used. Johannine terminology as well as the forms of thought and style which appear in the Fourth Gospel are genuinely Jewish and might not only go back to Jesus but also may be characteristic of his self-consciousness. The Johannine tradition has received its breadth in the apostle's teaching, but its substance was shaped by Jesus himself. Among the basic sayings, genuine *logia* uttered by Jesus and handed down in the Johannine tradition, the following ones might be mentioned: 3:3; 4:24, 34f, 37; 6:35, 56; 14:9; 15:5.

The fundamental agreement between the Synoptic and the Johannine traditions corroborates the historicity of the life, the activity and the message of Jesus. In their essence the two streams of tradition are identical.

Similar conclusions can be drawn from a study of the Farewell Discourses (chapters 13–17).[5] The evangelist by no means created his texts but was dependent upon and faithful to tradition which he expounded and shaped in a characteristic literary way. Jn 13:31 and 14:31 are significant proofs of the fact that there were different blocks of tradition, something that the evangelist was well aware of. The Farewell Discourses have many similarities of tradition and composition in common with the discourses in the Gospel of Matthew. The triad sin-righteousness-judgment in the sayings about the Paraclete (16:8–11) have a striking analogy in the triad justice-mercy-faith (Mt 23:23). In the exposition which is presented in Jn 16:8–11 we face three stages of development which resulted in the final shape of the text: tradition, interpretation and redaction.

In an article on the idea of mission in the Fourth Gospel,[6] Fridrichsen draws the following conclusion: What happens within the people of Israel has its consequences for the whole of mankind. Therefore the death of Jesus on the cross was not only an offering for the people (of Israel), 11:50; 18:14, but had the effect that the Lamb of God took away the sins of the world, 1:29. The Jewish people must perform a representative function in the world – an old Jewish concept. It has to serve mankind not only through its faith but also through its unbelief. The mission of the people of Israel is the prerequisite for the mission of the Christian Church with the aim of saving the whole world. This Johannine idea can be traced back to the way in which Jesus acted, according to the Synoptic gospels. In order to fulfil the universal mission of the Son of Man he confined his work and his earthly life to the lost sheep of the house of Israel (Mt 15:24; cf. 10:6).

[5] A. Fridrichsen, "Jesu avskedstal i fjärde evangeliet", *SEÅ* 3 (1938) 3–16.

[6] A. Fridrichsen, "Missionstanken i fjärde evangeliet", *SEÅ* 2 (1937) 137–148, cf. "Kyrkan i fjärde evangeliet", *Svensk Teologisk Kvartalskrift* 16 (1940) 27–42.

In one of his later essays Fridrichsen returned to the question as to whether the Gospel of John contains authentic tradition.[7] Once again he gave the answer that the core of this gospel, its basic elements, can beyond any doubt be supposed to possess their historical value independently of the Synoptic Gospels. The Johannine tradition of sayings (*logia*) is so homogeneous and simultaneously so consistant with the picture which the Synoptic Gospels give of the person and the activity of Jesus that its origin in a circle of disciples of Jesus cannot reasonably be doubted. It reflects the dominance of his person and his teaching. Whereas the tradition comes down from an eyewitness, the evangelist or redactor is anxious to retain in his gospel the portrait of Jesus which was alive in his church. The two gospel traditions are of equal value as sources for our knowledge of Jesus and complement each other. The Johannine tradition, however, provides a profounder interpretation of the person of Jesus and of his message: the revelation mediated by the Son who was sent to accomplish the Father's work in this world.

3. H. Odeberg

Having published his book on 3 Enoch, Odeberg turned to a subject connected with the New Testament. From the vast area of Rabbinic literature, from Mandaean sources and also from Hellenistic texts he drew parallels to passages in the Gospel of John.[8] All his findings are arranged in the form of a commentary. It is pity that this work was never completed. Only twelve chapters of the gospel have thus been illustrated by the immensurable fruits of Odeberg's extensive reading.

The author's main interest lies in early Jewish mysticism. "Normative" Rabbinism was by no means the exclusively and totally dominant religious sphere of the Palestinian Jews in the first centuries of our era. Within the environment of Rabbinical Judaism, mysticism lived its own life and can be found, with respect to central and constitutive tenants, to stand on the same side as Mandaeism, which probably was of Palestinian or near-Palestinian origin. Therefore, early Christianity and above all the Johannine writings should be viewed in relation not only to Rabbinical thinking but to Palestinian religious currents apart from Judaism. From this point of view a wealth of material has been collected from the Old Testament, the Septuagint, Rabbinic texts, Jewish literature written

[7] A. Fridrichsen, "Jesus, Johannes, Paulus", *En bok om bibeln*, (Lund, 1947) 148–179; = "Jesus, St John and St Paul", *The Root of the Vine* (ed. by A. G. Herbert, London, 1953) 37–62.

[8] H. Odeberg, *The Fourth Gospel* (Uppsala, 1929; reprinted Amsterdam, 1968) 336 pp.

in Greek, Mandaean sources, the Odes of Solomon, the *Corpus Hermeticum*, the so-called Mithras-Liturgy and other writings from that period. Only the Qumran library was not yet existant.

One of the passages which are dealt with at length is 3:13–21. Odeberg shows that 3:13 cannot be primarily directed against Jewish conceptions of the descent and ascent of the Shekinah but denies some theory of an ascent or of ascents into heaven, the assumption being that certain gifted or saintly men had ascended or could ascend on high although still on earth. Against this, the Fourth Gospel asserts that there is no ascent into heaven apart from that of the Son of Man. There is, however, an inclusive dimension in the figure of the Son of Man: those who are born from above are incorporated into the Son of Man and can ascend to heaven or enter the kingdom of God with or in the Son of Man. There is an identical conception in 2 Cor 12:2–4. Apart from the Son of Man there is no possibility of obtaining knowledge of or access to the heavenly world. The rise of faith within those who do the truth is connected with the arrival of the Light in this world, and the Light coming into the world is the Son of Man. All these ideas have their parallels in Jewish mysticism.

In this way Odeberg was able to show where the categories of thought and the terminology in which the Fourth Gospel expressed the Christian message had their roots. A deepened understanding of these roots is an indispensable help to the elimination of the language and the ideas of the gospel.

In an article published in Swedish and German Odeberg laid down some fundamental remarks on the methodology of Johannine studies.[9] He who works on the Fourth Gospel, must have an open and sensitive mind and be conscious of the depth of Johannine thought. The originality of the gospel as well as of its author must be respected. Influences and dependences can always be traced. But more important than acumen in detecting influences is an open mind for the uniqueness of the gospel and its message. There are backgrounds to the prologue and its details, but as a whole this chapter projects a concept of its own. Words can be taken over from a surrounding world, but this does not necessarily mean that there is an identity of ideas. Two different expressions such as "to be born from above" (3:3) and "a new creation" (2 Cor 5:17; Gal 6:15) can denote identical ideas, whereas significant terms such as life, death, flesh, spirit and faith in the Fourth Gospel can differ from

---

[9] H. Odeberg, "Über das Johannesevangelium", *Zeitschr. f. syst. Theol.* 16 (1939) 173–188; = "Johannesevangeliets krav på den teologiska forskningen", *Södermanlands bibelsällskaps årsbok* 1939, 3–17.

the same words use in Pauline letters. In this connection two separate questions are relevant: 1. Which was the Christian background of the gospel? 2. Which was the non-Christian background of the gospel? Hellenism and Palestinian Judaism are not exclusive alternatives. More adequate is a tripartition: Palestinian Judaism, Jewish dispersion, non-Jewish civilization. Already in the 1930's Odeberg was aware of the fact that Palestinian Judaism had been exposed to Hellenistic influences and that Jewish ideas had spread into the non-Jewish world. The aim of the Fourth Gospel was to unveil profound differences between Jesus and his opponents and thus to state more precisely the true originality of Jesus.

In a small paper from 1948 Odeberg refutes acutely the hypothesis that there had ever existed a second John (the presbyter) in Ephesus.[10] As was the case with later contributions from Odeberg[11] this paper has unfortunately never been published in another language than Swedish, which would have been worthwhile.

4. R. Gyllenberg

Throughout his later years Gyllenberg returned, in articles and commentaries, to problems in the Gospel of John.

Following Bultmann's outline of a development in primitive Christianity Gyllenberg traces back the origins of the Christian movement to four different groups of disciples of Jesus which contributed to the formation of characteristic traditions: Galilaean congregations, the Aramaic-speaking and the Hellenistic congregation in Jerusalem and finally groups within the baptist movement in the Jordan valley and other places in Judaea.[12] If this was the case, the beginnings of the Johannine tradition were as old as the origins of the Synoptic tradition. In the beginning there was a plurality.

The first collector of Johannine traditions chose to take his outlook from a place near the Jordan river. As this man seems to have been familiar with the area where baptist movements were active, he himself probably belonged to this kind of revival within the Jewish people. In this case the portrait of John the Baptist given in the Fourth Gospel is closer to reality than that given in the Synoptic Gospels. If Jesus had originally belonged to the baptist movement, the tension between him and the

---

[10] H. Odeberg, "Johannesevangeliets författare", *Erevna* 5 (1948) 151–156, cf. "Aposteln Johannes, Johannesevangeliets tillkomst, Johannesevangeliets syfte, Johannesevangeliets karaktär", *Erevna* 4 (1947) 81–114.

[11] H. Odeberg, "Om begreppet världen i Johannesevangeliet", *Erevna* 13 (1956) 39–41.

[12] R. Gyllenberg, "Die Anfänge der johanneischen Tradition", *Neutestamentliche Studien für Rudolf Bultmann* (Berlin, 1954) 144–147.

Baptist among disciples was a tension within this movement. In this case the criticism against official Judaism which is frequent in the Fourth Gospel can be of an early date and must not be attributed to a relatively late phase in the development of the Primitive Church.

Thoughtful attention was given to the structure of the gospel in question. At first sight it lacks a deliberate disposition and gives the impression of a chain of single elements. But soon it becomes evident that these elements have not been linked to each other at random.

According to Gyllenberg a characteristic feature of the Fourth Gospel is its cyclic structure,[13] the backbone of which is formed by the place-names. In this regard the gospel can be compared with the tunic of the Crucified which was woven in one piece throughout (19:23).

The cycles of events begin, each in its order, "beyond Jordan". The first cycle starts at 1:28 "beyond Jordan, where John was baptizing" and continues, as is the case also in the two following cycles, in Galilee. It ends up in Jerusalem, where Jesus cleanses the Temple and speaks of his coming death and resurrection (1:19–3:21). The second cycle reminds of that which happened beyond Jordan (3:26); it goes on through Samaria to Cana in Galilee and from there to Jerusalem (3:22–5:47). In the beginning of the third cycle Jesus withdraws to the farther shore of the Sea of Galilee (6:1), stays at Capernaum and in other parts of Galilee and returns to Jerusalem (6:1–10:39). The fourth cycle links up with the beginning of the gospel (10:40), but this time Jesus does not move to the north but to Bethany, from there to Ephraim, back to Bethany and then to Jerusalem. Also in this cycle Galilee has not been forgotten but appears in the final scenes (10:40–21:24). The last chapter is usually considered a later addition but is in fact, from the point of view of composition, an indispensable element.

The final events are grouped differently in comparison with the Synoptic Gospels.[14] The ascent to Jerusalem starts from the other side of Jordan (10:40). Jesus went, however, not up to the city itself but stopped at Bethany, where he raised Lazarus. This action had the effect that he was sentenced to death and had to disappear. Six days before the Jewish Passover he was at Bethany again (12:1), and there a crowd paid homage to him (12:12–19). Nothing is said about an entry into Jerusalem.

[13] R. Gyllenberg, "Cykliska element i Johannesevangeliets uppbyggnad", *[Finsk] Teologisk Tidskrift* 65 (1960) 309–315. See also *Johanneksen evankelium* (Helsinki, 1961) 380 pp. and "Evangelium enligt Johannes. Översättning och kommentar till valda stycken", *Religionspedagogiska institutets studiebibel* (ed. G. Lindeskog; Stockholm, 1980), 1, 177–237.

[14] R. Gyllenberg, "Intåget i Jerusalem och Johannesevangeliets uppbyggnad", *SEÅ* 41–42 (1977) 81–86.

According to this gospel, the public ministry was definitly brought to an end at Bethany.

The evangelist did not want to replace or to supplement the other stream of tradition. His interest was not historical but theological and kerygmatic. It is difficult to say where we get the most correct account of that which really happened. What the Fourth Gospel tells us about the last week in the life of Jesus sounds in any case reasonable.

The author of the Fourth Gospel shows a more critical attitude to his material than Mark.[15] The question is whether he had access to a more reliable tradition or whether he was sufficiently sensitive in sifting his material. A number of problems have received a better solution in his account. Certain similarities between the Christology of the Fourth Gospel, the traditions about the Messianic secret in Mark as viewed against the background of baptist movements point to a relatively early origin of the Johannine Tradition (which is not identical with the gospel).

An argument which stresses the authenticity of the information given in the Fourth Gospel is the fact that the gospel is familiar with the topography of Palestine. On the other hand, the single narratives are incomplete in a peculiar way.[16] This is the case with chapters 3, 4 and 11. There are perspicuous features in the conversations which the gospel relates. Against this, it can be said that a dialogue rarely comes to a precise end. Exactness and vagueness stand side by side.

There is not only a cyclic structure of the gospel as a whole. In addition to this the elements of the passion narrative are grouped in a symmetric way. Therefore the evangelist must have had a highly developed sense of structure and balance.

The three Scandinavian exegetes, whose obliging memory has been called to mind, have, each in his personal way, made lasting and trend-setting contributions to the study of the Gospel of John. They were firmly rooted in their time and in its scholarly work, and yet each one of them had his personal gifts and his originality and was thus able to transcend the limits and limitations of a stagnant consensus.

[15] R. Gyllenberg, "Johannesevangeliet som historisk källa", *SEÅ* 43 (1978) 74–86.
[16] R. Gyllenberg, *Åskådlighet och brist i åskådlighet i Fjärde evangeliet* (Societas Scientiarum Fennica, Årsbok, XLI B N.o 4; Helsinki, 1965), 15 pp; = "Anschauliches und Unanschauliches im vierten Evangelium", *ST* 21 (1967) 83–109.

Index of Passages

111